D1244158

ENGLISH CREAM-COLOURED EARTHENWARE

The Faber Monographs on Pottery and Porcelain
Edited by W. B. Honey and Arthur Lane

★

★

OTHER TITLES TO FOLLOW
Edited by Arthur Lane

A. *Coffee-pot. Height* 9¾ *in. Leeds. Circa* 1768.
Donald Towner. See page 19

ENGLISH CREAM-COLOURED EARTHENWARE

by

DONALD C. TOWNER

Honorary Secretary of the English Ceramic Circle

FABER AND FABER
24 Russell Square
London

First published in mcmlvii
by Faber and Faber Limited
24 Russell Square London W.C.1
Printed in Great Britain by
R. MacLehose and Company Limited
The University Press Glasgow

To
BERNARD RACKHAM

FOREWORD

The two great discoveries in eighteenth-century European ceramics were porcelain and 'cream-coloured earthenware'. The latter was an original English invention, which in the hands of Wedgwood and his contemporaries at Leeds and elsewhere practically superseded porcelain and the more old-fashioned delftware. Its cheapness and convenience won for it a huge export trade, and factories all over Europe began making wares of 'English type'.

The world-wide success of English creamware was largely due to the novelty and elegance of its shapes; these embodied the new neo-classical taste of which Wedgwood and the brothers Adam were the leading exponents. Its eminently practical qualities, on the other hand, were the fruit of a sound tradition in Staffordshire, where creamware can now be seen to have developed naturally from saltglaze and the earthenwares associated with the great Thomas Whieldon. Mr. Towner, who is Honorary Secretary of the English Ceramic Circle and a practising artist, has devoted many years of study to a subject which has been unaccountably neglected—perhaps because early records were so hard to find. By close stylistic comparison of the objects in the light of the documents he has now been able to classify the work of the different creamware factories, adding a new chapter to the history of the potter's art in England. The beauty of the objects will be a revelation to the many who are unfamiliar with them. And their importance may be judged by the fact that they were the first wares to be made by the methods of modern industry—the direct ancestors of the household china we use today.

ARTHUR LANE

ACKNOWLEDGEMENTS

I wish to express my gratitude to Mr. Arthur Lane for his valuable assistance as editor, also to Sir John Wedgwood for the helpful facilities given me for research into the Wedgwood manuscripts at Barlaston and for permission to publish letters and other records from these documents. My thanks are also due to the following museums for the great help given me, from time to time, in the examination of exhibits and for their permission to have some of them photographed for inclusion in this book:

British Museum, London (Plates I, 8A, 11, 12, 75B).

Victoria and Albert Museum, London (Plates 3A, B, 4, 6B, 7A, 19B, 21, 23A, B, 39, 51A, 54, 58, 61, 65A, 70, 75A, 76A, 82B, 86A, 90B, 91A, B.)

Fitzwilliam Museum, Cambridge (Plates 6A, 10, 24, 26A, 49, 69, 88B, 93, 94).

Leeds City Art Gallery and Temple Newsam House (Plates 9A, 33, 38, 42A, 44, 45, 47).

Castle Museum, Norwich (Plates 64B, 77B, 79A); and to the Hanley Museum, Stoke-on-Trent, for permission to publish extracts from Thomas Whieldon's notebook. I also wish to thank the following collectors for their kindness in allowing me to illustrate pieces from their collections:

Mr. and Mrs. Victor Gollancz (Plates 2B, 5, 13B, 18B, 19A, 25, 30A, B, 41A, 55, 60, 62B, 63A, B, 66B, 67, 80A).

Mrs. H. McLeod (Plate 22B).

The trustees of the late Mr. T. Murray Ragg (Plates 72, 78A, 80B, 81).

Mrs. Robert Sargeant (Plates 53A, B, 82A).

Miss Margaret Thomas (Plate 90A); and Mr. A. T. Morley Hewitt, for permission to publish a drawing from a shard in his collection (Appendix I, Plate VI, fig. 3).

D. C. T.

CONTENTS

CONTENTS

xiv

ILLUSTRATIONS

COLOUR PLATES

MONOCHROME PLATES

at the end of the book

1

INTRODUCTION

Cream-Coloured Earthenware, usually known by the shortened form of Cream-colour or Creamware, was the direct descendant of the lead-glazed wares of the Middle Ages. English pottery, through the ages, had become successively more refined, more technically perfect and more artistically excellent until it reached its climax in the creamware of the eighteenth century with its fine form, thin body, clean and brilliant glaze which formed a perfect background for the ingenious, harmonious and free painting of the earthenware enamellers of that time. It was the prototype of the lead-glazed earthenware that is manufactured today, though standardization and mass production have largely destroyed its charm, individuality and beauty of potting and design. At its best it did not seek to imitate porcelain either in colour, form, or decoration, but remained essentially true to its English earthenware tradition. Even when the creamware potters sought inspiration from the work of the silversmith, the metal forms were freely adapted to form a more plastic idiom suitable to the clay medium. So traditional was the creamware that it would be truer to say that it evolved from the main stream of English pottery than that it was invented at any particular time.

Earthenware that was cream in colour was made from the begin-ning of the eighteenth century. At first the potters coated a darker body with a cream-coloured slip, but by the importation of clays from Devonshire together with the introduction of calcined flint in 1720 the manufacture of creamware was made possible. This discovery is us-ually ascribed to John Astbury of Shelton, though Josiah Wedgwood attributes it to Heath of Shelton. These materials when fired to a temperature high enough to form a stoneware produced the white saltglazed ware or 'white stoneware' as it used to be called. Salt, which was thrown into the kiln during the process of firing, volatilized and formed a vitreous silicate on the surface of the ware. The same materials, however, when fired to a lower temperature and glazed with lead, formed the Cream-Coloured Earthenware. This was probably first produced by Thomas Astbury some time between 1720 and

1740.[1] At this time the lead powder or galena, mixed with a certain amount of ground flint, was dusted on the ware, which was then given its one and only firing. This process produced an extremely brilliant transparent glaze of a rich cream colour. Small stamped motifs similar to those found on saltglaze and red ware were often applied to the cream colour of this time. Dry crystals of metallic oxides such as copper, iron and manganese, were frequently dusted on, probably with the tip of a brush. These dissolved during the firing and mixing with the lead ran in a charming, but somewhat uncontrolled manner, to form touches of coloured decoration (I). This form of decoration led directly to the 'tortoiseshell' and other wares with coloured glazes. The method employed at this time of producing the cream-coloured ware was found to be unsatisfactory as the lead powder produced poisoning among the potters, and the grinding of the flint stones a disease known as potter's rot. Patents were therefore taken out between 1726 and 1732 for grinding the flint stones in water, and about 1740 a fluid glaze was invented, probably by Enoch Booth of Tunstall, Staffordshire, in which the lead and flint were both mixed and ground in water. The method was adopted of first firing the ware to a biscuit, and then glazing and re-firing it. The date usually given for this invention is 1750, but in actual fact it must have taken place about ten years earlier (see page 5). Having described the chief developments which resulted in the double-fired creamware coated with a fluid glaze it must be pointed out that this did not immediately displace the previous types. Thus creamware with small applied reliefs touched in with underglaze colours was made at least as late as 1761, the year of the marriage of King George III, which event was sometimes depicted on this type of ware. Tortoiseshell and other wares with coloured glazes as well as saltglazed stoneware continued to be made in quantity till late in the century, so that much of the double fired creamware was made before many specimens of types which preceded it.

Between the years 1743 and 1750 great developments were made in the creamware. By 1750 the ware was already being enamelled and had a rapidly increasing market which during the next few years was to spread to the Continent as well. At this time the creamware was being made by the saltglaze potters, and painted by the saltglaze enamellers. Much of it, therefore, bore a strong resemblance to the

---

[1] Some small creamware teapots decorated with coffee-coloured applied stamped ornaments similar in pattern to those found on some early saltglazed stoneware, may perhaps be attributable to Thomas Astbury. Examples of this type of creamware are at the Castle Museum, Norwich.

(I) *Plates* 3A, B, 4.

saltglaze ware both in form and decoration. Teapots were globular in shape with crabstock handles and spouts (1); coffee-pots were pear-shaped with magnificent upright spouts and flat-looped handles with pinched ends (2). The colour was a deep cream almost amounting to buff and was derived not only from the body but also from the glaze, the latter usually being either a deep yellow, a soft brown or a bright lemon-yellow with a tinge of green, though one of the earliest glazes on creamware was of a bluish tint. As would be expected, it was during this early period of the ware that the greatest vigour, freedom and originality were shown, while the full possibilities of the material were as yet undiscovered. Foremost of the pioneers in Staffordshire who availed themselves of Enoch Booth's invention were Thomas Whieldon and John Warburton. The creamware was not, however, confined to Staffordshire; in fact it has become evident that saltglaze potters were working in a number of large potting centres outside Staffordshire such as Derby, Liverpool and Leeds, and wherever this was so, the manufacture of creamware was developed to the eventual exclusion of the saltglazed stoneware.

By 1751 an improved creamware is stated to have been made by the Warburtons. Ten years later Josiah Wedgwood was directing all his efforts towards its development and by 1763 he was producing a considerably refined ware of a much paler colour. By 1768 he had transformed the creamware into virtually a new substance of great beauty, which combined lightness with strength and was capable of the greatest delicacy of workmanship. There were no doubt many contributing factors towards this great change in the creamware, but first and foremost was the introduction of china-clay and china-stone from Cornwall, into the body and glaze. The glaze used by Wedgwood at this time was a yellowish-green colour which may be seen in crevices where it lies more thickly. By 1770 other Staffordshire creamware potters were producing the light-coloured creamware to which Wedgwood had given the name 'Queen's Ware'. The Yorkshire potters on the other hand continued to make the deeper-coloured creamware for some years afterwards, probably till 1775. The letter from Wedgwood on page 34 shows that the creamware potteries, at this time at any rate, made either the deep or pale creamware, but were unable for practical reasons to make both simultaneously. Only a few minor changes in the development of creamware were made after this. Of importance, however, was a considerable increase about 1780 in the production of creamware, the glaze of which was tinged with blue. This glaze when applied to a somewhat modified creamware body pro-

(1) *Plate* 8A ; (2) *Plate* 5.

duced a cool grey-coloured ware and is usually referred to as 'pearl-ware'. In this type of ware the blue glaze was always at variance with the warm-coloured body and was therefore less satisfactory than the green or yellow glazes, though Neale of Hanley and the Leeds Pottery produced some very pleasing pearlware of a fine quality.

The difficulty of attributing pieces of creamware to a particular factory has always been of the greatest difficulty as virtually no creamware was marked prior to Josiah Wedgwood's manufacture of it in Burslem about 1761. In 1772 Wedgwood wrote to Thomas Bentley proposing that all his ware should be marked, but even after that date a considerable quantity seems to have missed being stamped. Other factories were for the most part content to leave their ware unmarked. Another difficulty lies in the similarity of both body and glaze of the creamware made by a number of potteries; shapes and designs were freely copied or interchanged; similar pattern books were issued by several creamware factories, and identical moulds in some cases used. Nor can we be helped to any great extent by the enamelled decoration, as with but a few exceptions factories sent their creamware to outside enamellers for decoration so that one enameller might decorate the ware of a number of potters. The practice of enamelling creamware at the factory itself was only gradually adopted. It follows therefore, that there is a great deal in the present subject that awaits confirmation and further discovery. It must be pointed out, however, that little progress can be made unless the whole field of creamware manufacture is kept in view.

2

PIONEERS

ENOCH BOOTH

Master Potter at Tunstall, Staffordshire

Enoch Booth was a saltglaze potter who decorated his ware with that form of decoration known as 'scratch-blue'. Fortunately he signed and dated some of his ware; and it should be noted that he was one of the very few saltglaze potters who ever did so. This may be an indication of the experimental nature of his work. A scratch-blue saltglaze mug in the Glaisher Collection at Cambridge is inscribed 'Enoch Booth 1742' (see Mark 1, page 86)[1] A loving cup also in scratch-blue saltglaze at the Hanley Museum is inscribed 'E.B. 1750' (see Mark 2, page 86).[2] A creamware punch-bowl in the British Museum is inscribed 'E.B. 1743' (see Mark 3, page 86) (1). There is very little doubt that this punch-bowl was also made by Enoch Booth, and from what has already been said it is apparent that he continued his manufacture of saltglaze while experimenting with the new creamware. This magnificent bowl which is 10 inches in diameter is painted in underglaze blue in reserved panels between which on the outside is a ground finely speckled with manganese-purple. As it is impossible to produce ware decorated with underglaze blue painting by employing a single firing only, it is certain that the double fired creamware was already in existence by the year 1743. No other example of creamware by Enoch Booth has yet been identified with certainty, but some experimental pieces, with underglaze blue painting (sometimes over an incised decoration reminiscent of scratch-blue saltglaze) or with manganese-painted decoration, may possibly be of his make.

[1] Illustrated in Bernard Rackham, *Early Staffordshire Pottery*, London, 1951, Plate 54.

[2] Illustrated in J. C. Wedgwood, *Staffordshire Pottery and its History*, London, 1914, facing page 68.

(1) *Plate* 1A, B, 2A.

ENGLISH CREAM-COLOURED EARTHENWARE

THOMAS WHIELDON

Born at Stoke 1719; Master Potter at Fenton Hall, Staffordshire, 1740; died 1795

Rightly or wrongly a great many different kinds of ware have been attributed to the great potter Thomas Whieldon, but he has seldom been given the credit for making creamware. Yet an item in his notebook in the Hanley Museum reads as follows:

Mr. THOMAS FLETCHER Dr.

Nov. 7. 1749.

1 doz. plates	Tor.	—	8/-
2 doz. do.	plane	—	
1 doz. do.	painted	—	2/-
1 doz. do.	Cream Colr.		1/8
5 pails	—		2/6

'Tor' in the first item is an abbreviation frequently used by Whieldon for 'Tortoiseshell'. At first sight '2 doz. do. plane' looks as though it might refer to creamware, in which case the following item would suggest that this was sometimes painted, and this may be so. But the following item definitely states 'Cream Colour', so that the foregoing may refer to saltglaze, though Whieldon usually refers to this as 'white-ware' or 'white stoneware'. However that may be, we have the statement that he was manufacturing the cream-colour in 1749 and further that some of his ware bore painted decoration.

'Painting' might refer to either enamel decoration, or to painting under the glaze. Except that the idea is so revolutionary, the obvious inference would be that the plates in question were painted in enamel colours. With regard to painting in metallic glazes, pieces of tortoiseshell ware in an unfinished state, which were found at Fenton Low during excavations there, show that metallic colours were applied to the ware in the biscuit state, and that the subsequent glazing and firing caused these to melt and merge into one another. Under no circumstances, therefore, could tortoiseshell or mottled-ware be referred to as painted ware. A few pieces exist, however, the decorations of which consist of skilful figure-painting, in which manganese and other metallic glazes are used with a brush under the glaze. The beautiful teapot illustrated (1) is almost certainly by Whieldon. It is painted in brown, green and yellow (manganese, copper and iron) under the glaze. The knob, handle, spout and feet are of solid agate ware. If, however, this was the kind of painting referred to by Whiel-

(1) *Plate* 2B.

don in the bill quoted, one would expect the price of the plates in question to be at least as high as those with tortoiseshell decoration, instead of which it is only one-quarter the amount. Though not conclusive it would be reasonable to admit the possibility of Whieldon having used enamel painting on saltglaze or creamware, and if the one, then probably also the other.

Entries in Whieldon's notebook show that he owned the pot-works at Fenton Low and some land round about it. He probably worked there himself in his early days (though there appears to be no absolute proof of this); but if so, he had moved out by 1750, as from that date until 1762 the pot-works was let continuously to other potters, their names, the amount of rents received and dates being recorded in the notebook. In 1759 Whieldon was certainly working at Fenton Hall in the same neighbourhood.[1] Since 1900, a number of excavations have been made on the site of the Fenton Low pot-works, but out of hundreds of fragments discovered, only a very few were of creamware and of these only one is likely to have been made before 1750, and therefore perhaps by Whieldon himself; this is a creamware teapot cover with a bird knob, now in the Victoria and Albert Museum. It is a rich cream colour with a finely-crazed golden glaze. The other pieces of creamware found could all be dated as having been made between 1760 and 1770 or even later and are therefore valueless as indications of Whieldon's work. They include a shell pattern teapot spout (Castle Museum, Norwich), identical with that on a teapot in the author's collection (1); a portion of a teapot in the Morley Hewitt collection showing handle terminals very similar to those made at Leeds (see Appendix I, Plate VI, fig. 3); as well as a few specimens with green-glazed stripes, a type of which nearly all the surviving complete examples were made at Leeds, some specimens bearing the Leeds Pottery mark.

At first Whieldon's creamware is likely to have been made in shapes similar to his tortoiseshell or saltglaze ware. Plates would probably be octagonal (a shape described as 'square' in early account books); jugs and coffee-pots would have handles of the flat loop variety with pinched end (Appendix I, Plate III, figs. 2, 2A); teapot handles and spouts would be either crabstock (Appendix I, Plate III, fig. 1) or facetted (Appendix I, Plate III, fig. 5). We should expect the glaze in

[1] Wedgwood in his 'Experiment Book' writes: 'This suite of experiments was begun at Fenton Hall, in the parish of Stoke-on-Trent, about the beginning of the year 1759, in my partnership with Mr. Whieldon, for the improvement of our manufacture of earthenware . . .', etc.

(1) *Plate 77*A.

some cases to have been very finely crazed, and the colour a rich cream.

At present no piece of creamware either plain or painted can be attributed to Whieldon with absolute certainty, but the following pieces are given as likely examples of his work:

1. Teapot, referred to on page 6; c. 1743 (1).
2. Double tea-caddy with a space for tea-spoons or a drawer to contain them, in tortoiseshell ware; c. 1745 (2).
3. Similar double tea-caddy in plain creamware; c. 1745 (3). A plate with similar moulded pattern decorated in underglaze colours is in the Victoria and Albert Museum.
4. Sugar-bowl in tortoiseshell ware with a bird knob similar to the one found at Fenton Low already mentioned; c. 1750 (4).
5. Sugar-bowl similar to the above but in plain creamware with applied and gilded decoration; c. 1750 (5).
6. Jug, enamelled by Robinson and Rhodes of Leeds, and therefore perhaps bought by them in the white; c. 1765 (6).
7. Coffee-pot, painted in enamel colours probably in Staffordshire; c. 1755 (7). Compare the spout of this pot with that shown on Plate 4.[1]
8. Candlestick with the same groundwork as the caddies (a) and (b). This consists of repeated impressions of a circle with a dot in the centre made by a tool; c. 1765 (8).

THE WARBURTONS OF HOT LANE, COBRIDGE, STAFFORDSHIRE
John Warburton 1720–61; *Anne Warburton* (*née Daniel*), 1713–98;
Master Potter 1761

Soon after 1740, Cobridge became the centre of the enamelling industry which sprang into existence when it was discovered that the fine white saltglaze formed a suitable surface for enamel painting. At first enamelling on saltglaze and creamware was a specialized industry, and in some cases the potter might have to send his ware a considerable distance to be enamelled. The Warburtons of Hot Lane, Cobridge, were an exception to this, for they are reputed to have been not only pioneers of creamware manufacture but also enamellers of considerable ability.

John Warburton married Anne Daniel. The Daniels were a neigh-

[1] The possibility of both these coffee-pots having been made either by Wedgwood or at the Leeds Pottery cannot be overlooked. They are identical in shape and detail to some in unglazed red-ware, which was made at both of these factories.

(1) *Plate* 2B; (2) *Plate* 6A; (3) *Plate* 6B; (4) *Plate* 7A; (5) *Plate* 7B; (6) *Plate* 20; (7) *Plate* 5; (8) *Plate* 50A (i).

bouring family of enamellers also of Hot Lane, Cobridge.[1] After John's death in 1761, Anne became master potter.

In his *History of the Staffordshire Potteries* published in 1829, Simeon Shaw states, 'In 1751 were the last improvements of Cream Colour (prior to those of the late Mr. Wedgwood) by Mrs. Warburton of Hot Lane.' Also, 'Mr. Wedgwood employed a waggon once a fortnight to take down a load of cream colour to be printed by Messrs. Sadler and Green of Liverpool . . . the teaware required to be painted was sent to Mrs. Warburton in Hot Lane and some time elapsed before Mr. Wedgwood had the enamelling done on his own premises.' In spite of this indication, not one example of Anne Warburton's creamware or enamelling can now be identified. There is no doubt that the Warburtons were potters of repute. Bills showing the sale of their creamware to Josiah Wedgwood are amongst the records kept at Barlaston, but no mention of their enamelling is made, whereas a number of other enamellers are mentioned in the correspondence as doing work for Wedgwood from 1763 onwards (see page 35). Josiah C. Wedgwood in his book *Staffordshire Pottery and its History* suggests, probably correctly, that much of the Warburton creamware is erroneously attributed to Josiah Wedgwood.

Many descendants of John and Anne Warburton became potters of repute. Among these, their son Jacob (1741–1826) became one of the original partners of the New Hall works, while Peter and Francis Warburton,[2] grandsons of John and Anne, manufactured some very fine creamware which was a rich cream in colour with a yellowish glaze. Some pieces are marked 'P and F. Warburton', either in capitals or in lower-case lettering (Appendix III, Marks 129, 130, 131). Some remarkably fine cruets, with well-modelled figures[3] forming the centre, can be ascribed to them. A marked example is in the collection at the Leeds Art Gallery. Some white-ware vases in the neo-classical style marked 'WARBURTON' impressed, were made about the end of the eighteenth century; but from which branch of the Warburton family they originated, is uncertain.

[1] Very little is known of the productions of the Daniels. A cake-basket of fine quality creamware and signed 'John Daniel, 1775' is at the British Museum (Appendix III, Mark 101). John Daniel (1756–1821) was the son of Ralph Daniel of Cobridge, and nephew to Anne Warburton.

[2] Francis Warburton set up a factory—La Charité-sur-Loire, Nièvre, France, in 1802 (see page 62).

[3] Unmarked figures from the same moulds as those forming the centre of the Warburton cruets, but having square bases and enamelled in colours are sometimes found.

COCKPIT HILL, DERBY

This factory was founded about 1750 by John Heath. The following year a deed of partnership was signed between John Heath, William Butts, Thomas Rivett and Ralph Steane to commence making pottery at Cockpit Hill. In 1779 John and Christopher Heath were bankrupt and the next year all the existing stock was sold. Thus the life of the factory was barely thirty years.[1]

The following is an advertisement in the *Derby Mercury* of the 17th, 24th and 31st of March 1780, for the sale of the stock-in-trade of the pot works after the bankruptcy.

'To the Merchants, Traders and Dealers in Earthenware. To be sold without reserve (and considerably under the usual Wholesale Price). At the Derby Pot Manufactury, A large quantity of Earthenware, being the whole stock in trade of that great and extensive factory commonly known by the name of Derby Pot Works, consisting of an assortment of enamell'd and blue and white useful China: a large quantity of Enamelled Cream Ware, and plain Cream tentable ware; a great quantity of White stone and Brown Ware. N.B. The aforesaid Earthenware etc. will be opened for sale on the 4th and 6th of April and continue selling every Tuesday and Thursday until the whole is disposed of on which days (but no others in the week) a proper person will attend the Sale.

'This Earthenware will be sold in different lots and is well worth the notice of Pot Carriers in and about the neighbourhood of Coleorton Moor.

'No less a quantity than two horse loads will be sold to one person.'

From this advertisement it is evident that the Derby Pot Works produced plain and enamelled creamware amongst other products which included 'white stone', i.e. saltglaze, and brown-ware, which was probably similar to the Nottingham saltglazed stoneware.

The word 'tentable' in the advertisement is probably a printer's error for 'teatable'.

An 'assortment of Blue and White China' probably refers to china

[1] See F. Williamson, *The Derby Pot Manufactory known as Cockpit Hill*, Derby, 1931; and also Geoffrey Godden, 'Derby Pot Works, Cockpit Hill' in *Transactions of the English Ceramic Circle*, Vol. III, Part IV, 1955.

of other makes, as it is known that the Cockpit Hill factory also bought and sold 'all sorts of wares belonging to ye art of making china' (Jewitt), whereas creamware and saltglaze are specified as being in 'large' and 'great' quantities respectively, and were no doubt the chief products of the factory.

In 1764 John Heath and William Duesbury acquired the process of printing from Richard Holdship,[1] and it is through the marked transfer-printed ware that we have become acquainted with the Cockpit Hill creamware generally. That the marks are printed and not incised or impressed is of course unsatisfactory, but all the marked pots are so consistent in character, design, potting and glazing that there is no doubt whatever that they are all of one manufacture, and it is hardly conceivable that they could have been made by any other factory than Cockpit Hill.

The following marked pieces are now known:

1. Teapot in the British Museum (1), height 4 inches; globular; facetted spout; ribbed loop handle (the ribs are barely visible owing to bad moulding); knob, flat and round on a very short stem, like a button, pierced through the centre to form a steam-hole. The pot has a very slight outward turn at the base, suggesting a diminutive foot-rim. The glaze is a dirty yellow, badly crazed all over. A noticeable feature of the crazing is a tendency for it to run in strong horizontal lines. The vertical cracks are generally less marked. Though the glaze is brilliant, the general appearance is somewhat dirty, and it is probable that originally the glaze was a bright greenish-yellow which has become stained in use. On one side is a version of the 'Tea party', transfer-printed in black, and marked in the print 'Radford Sc. Derby Pot Works'. On the reverse is a print of the 'Push-cart' signed 'Pot

[1] Richard Holdship, from 1751 till 1759, was a partner in the Worcester porcelain factory where he was mainly concerned with the transfer-printing, but in what capacity is uncertain. An anchor for 'hold-ship' is supposed to be his rebus. This occurs both on Worcester transfer-prints sometimes combined with the name Hancock (the Worcester engraver) as well as on some Cockpit Hill transfer-printed creamware combined with the word 'Derby'. 'Radford sculpsit Derby Pot works' also occurs on Cockpit Hill creamware but no specimen has yet been found on which the name 'Radford' and the anchor mark both occur in combination upon the same print. It would be reasonable therefore to ascribe those pieces which have the anchor mark to Richard Holdship, though it is by no means certain that he did any actual engraving himself, whereas it is certain that Radford was the engraver of those prints marked with his name and there is such a close approximation of style between all the Cockpit Hill engravings as to suggest that they were by the same hand, and therefore by Thomas Radford. The subjects of the Cockpit Hill transfer-printing were largely derived from engravings printed on Worcester porcelain. (See Cyril Cook, *The Life and Work of Robert Hancock*, London, 1948.)

(1) *Plates* 11A, B.

Works in Derby'. On the cover is a print of three cherubs within a husk border.

2. Teapot in the Glaisher collection at the Fitzwilliam Museum, Cambridge (1), height 4½ inches; globular with the greatest width slightly above the centre; facetted spout showing traces of small moulded pattern (Appendix I, Plate I, fig. 2); scroll handle (Appendix I, Plate III, fig. 3B); knob, a formalized upright flower. The glaze is a brilliant greenish-yellow, crazed in strong horizontal lines and is speckled with sanding. The underside is unglazed and has a circular concavity in the centre about 1 inch in diameter and ⅛ inch in depth. Transfer-printed in black, on one side 'L'amour', on the reverse a combination of 'Tea Party' and 'Push-cart'. Marked in the print with an anchor and 'Derby' (Appendix III, Mark 6).

3. Jug in the possession of Franklin Barret, Esq.,[1] height 4 inches; flat loop handle with pinched end. The glaze is a bright greenish-yellow, crazed all over with a strong horizontal tendency, and is very unevenly and badly applied. Transfer-printed in black on one side 'L'amour'; on the reverse 'The garden conversation'; marked in the print with an anchor and 'Derby' (Appendix III, Mark 6).

4. Teapot in the Derby Museum and Art Gallery,[1] height 4¼ inches; globular with the greatest width slightly above the centre; facetted spout; ribbed loop handle; pierced button knob; transfer-printed in black, on one side a portrait bust of Catherine II of Russia surrounded by an inscription in Rusian, marked in the print 'T. Radford Sc. Derby'. On the reverse the Russian arms with the date 1765 and the words 'Rouble Coin' on either side, the whole surrounded by a floral border. The cover is decorated with two floral sprays.

5. Plate in the collection of C. L. Exley, Esq.,[2] six-lobed 'Royal Pattern'; diameter 8¼ inches; clumsily potted with bright greenish-yellow glaze unevenly applied and badly crazed, the crazing running in long uneven lines; transfer-printed with two lovers seated under a tree watching two dogs at play, under the inscription 'Summer Amusements'. Three groups of flowers round the rim, marked in the print with an anchor and the word 'Derby' (Appendix III, Mark 6).

6. Plate in the collection of C. L. Exley Esq.,[2] six-lobed 'Royal Pattern'; diameter 8¼ inches; similar to No. 5, but decorated with a print of 'L'amour' and the words 'French Amour'. It is marked with

---

[1] Illustrated in Geoffrey Godden, 'Derby Pot Works, Cockpit Hill', in *Transactions of the English Ceramic Circle*, Vol. III, Part IV, London, 1955; on Plate 67A and Plate 68B, C.

[2] Ibid., Plates 65C, D.

an anchor and the word 'Derby' in print. (Appendix III, Mark 6.)

7. Teapot in the Willett Collection, Brighton. Transfer-printed in black with a portrait of John Wilkes on one side; signed 'T. Radford' in the print.

From these seven pieces the characteristics of Cockpit Hill cream-ware can be enumerated as follows:

1. A brilliant glaze, which is bright greenish-yellow in colour.

2. The glaze is often crazed and sometimes shows evidence of sand-ing; the crazing has a tendency to run in long lines in places; else-where it forms a fairly even mesh.

3. The potting and general workmanship are often rather poor.

4. The spouts are often facetted.

5. The knobs are often like a button, and are pierced for the steam-hole.

6. The greatest width of the teapots is slightly above the centre.

7. The undersides of pots are usually unglazed and sometimes have a central concavity about 1 inch in diameter. (The undersides are sometimes partially glazed where the glaze has run accidentally.)

8. Scroll handles are cut off square and not divided into two lobes as in the Wedgwood variety.

A number of examples of enamelled creamware with the above characteristics are known, though the general quality and workman-ship of these is usually superior to those of the transfer-printed pieces. It cannot be sufficiently emphasized, however, that the shapes of handles, spouts or knobs are insufficient in themselves as grounds for attribution to the Cockpit Hill factory. These should be used as pointers only, as it is probable that some of the Cockpit Hill shapes were derived from those made in Staffordshire at an early date. But when other characteristics also agree, an attribution can be made with confidence. It is very probable that many saltglaze teapots, etc., with facetted spouts were the products of the Cockpit Hill factory.

The creamware teapot with enamelled flower decoration in red, black and green (I) corresponds in every respect, except for the decoration, with the marked transfer-printed teapot in the Glaisher collection already described (Note No. 2, page 12). It has a brilliant glaze which is bright greenish-yellow in colour and is badly crazed in long running lines. It is badly sanded, unglazed underneath, and the scroll handle is cut off square at the base and not divided. Underneath are four black strokes and a green spot, which were probably made by the enameller in trying out his colours.

(I) *Plate* 8B.

Another teapot (1) height 4 inches, has some very direct and charming painting of birds, and is of much better quality generally than the transfer-printed pieces though possessing the usual characteristics of glaze, crazing, etc. It is also unglazed underneath, with a central concavity. The long running lines of crazing are very discernible. This teapot introduces a different type of spout (Appendix I, Plate I, fig. 6). The scroll handle has the typical Cockpit Hill square end. The enamelling is in soft Indian red, black and green; on the reverse side is some delicate and charming flower-painting. This and the beautiful coffee-pot (2), which is of Leeds origin, were painted by an enameller whose decorations on Derby porcelain are well known.

The teapot with the inscription 'Harper for Ever' (3) is in the British Museum, and is there ascribed to Cockpit Hill on the grounds of its inscription. Harper was elected Member of Parliament for Derby in 1761, but failed in the election of 1768. This teapot was probably made to celebrate his success in 1761, and one would expect a local product to be used for such a purpose and occasion. The style and deeper cream colour of this teapot, point to its being of an earlier date than the foregoing Derby pots. It has, however, two features in common with the later Derby teapots, namely, its greatest width above the centre, and a modified foot-rim.

The teapot with the inscription 'Wilkes & Liberty' (4) at Temple Newsam House, Leeds, possesses all the dominant features of the foregoing painted or printed pots but is of very fine quality.

From these and other painted creamware of Derby origin it becomes apparent that the Cockpit Hill factory had a very large output, and that its wares varied very much in quality. Some of its transfer-printed wares are very poor, but some of its enamelled wares are of such superb quality as to rank among the finest examples of creamware. The enamelling differs from that on creamware of other factories. The green is usually a thick bluish-green; the blue is a soft grey-blue; and the red is usually an Indian red as compared with the Venetian red used on other creamware, though the finely painted roses, honeysuckle, and cherries on some early pieces are much paler in colour.

After the close of the Cockpit Hill factory, some creamware was made between 1780 and 1785 at the Nottingham Road factory, Derby. This ware is reputed to have been of fine quality, but has not yet been identified.

---

(1) *Plate* 9B; (2) *Plate* 25; (3) *Plate* 8A; (4) *Plate* 9A.

4

THE LEEDS POTTERY

Of a group of potteries which existed in Yorkshire in the eighteenth century the most important was situated in Jack Lane, Hunslet, and was known as the 'Leeds Pottery'. It was founded some time prior to 1758, when it was mentioned in local records. It is believed that two brothers named Green, probably John and Joshua, who were partners in 1775, became the proprietors in 1760; and it may be that cream-ware was first made at Leeds about this date. There is a tradition that delftware was made here at one time, but it is certain that the manu-facture of fine white saltglaze (1), unglazed red-ware, tortoiseshell and other types of ware with coloured glazes were made at Leeds in quantity, till about 1780. Pearlware, i.e. creamware with a bluish glaze, was introduced at Leeds about 1785 and black basalt ware at the end of the century, but the ware for which the pottery became so justly famous was the creamware. In 1770 the Leeds pottery was con-siderably enlarged, and at this time was trading under the name 'Humble, Green & Co.'. Between 1775 and 1780, with William Hartley as the leading partner, the firm became 'Humble, Hartley, Greens & Co.' and in 1781 'Hartley, Greens & Company'.

Jewitt in *Ceramic Art of Great Britain* states that in the year 1791 the output of the Leeds pottery had become so great that the yearly balance then struck amounted to over £51,500. At this time an enor-mous export trade was carried on with the Continent, not only by the Leeds pottery but by Wedgwood, John Turner of Lane End, and other English factories. The Continental factories in self-defence turned from the manufacture of Faïence to that of creamware which they made in imitation of the English,[1] and it may have been this more than anything else that proved to be the undoing of the Leeds pottery, which became bankrupt in 1820, shortly after the death of William Hartley. After this date the pottery changed hands a number of times till it was finally closed down in 1878, but little of ceramic interest was made after the Hartley, Greens period.

[1] See *Continental Creamware*, p. 59.

(1) *Plates* 42A, 45.

The early creamware of the Leeds pottery has not been positively known until very recently. In the past a large group of beautiful creamware of a very deep cream colour, either plain or enamelled in red and black sometimes with touches of green, has been assumed to be the early Leeds creamware on the strength of certain similarities and characteristics which occur both on the ware of this group and of the later group of light coloured creamware, some pieces of which bear the Leeds Pottery impressed mark. This assumption has proved to have been correct, as pieces of the early group have now been found bearing the impressed mark of the Leeds Pottery. At Leeds the change-over from the early deep colouring to the pale tone of the later creamware took place in 1775, while at some Staffordshire potteries the change had occurred before this date. The creamware made by the Leeds Pottery between the years 1760 and 1775 still possessed something of the ruggedness of a peasant craft combined with a strength, vigour and beauty of form quite alien to any kind of sophistication but which often showed a technical achievement of the highest order.

The shell sweet-meat dish (1) is an early piece of buff-coloured creamware. It is marked 'LEEDS*POTTERY' (Appendix III, Mark 7) and in body and glaze corresponds exactly with other pieces made before 1775. Other examples also correspond exactly and link up with the whole group of early Leeds creamware.

As already stated on page 3, the introduction of china-clay and stone from Cornwall into the body and glaze of the creamware took place later in Yorkshire than in Staffordshire. At Leeds this seems to have taken place in 1775 when the patent restrictions on these materials were removed as far as the making of earthenware was concerned. (It would seem that some Staffordshire potters had a right to their use previously, in spite of the patent.) The incorporation of china-clay and stone into the creamware virtually transformed it into a new material, making it at once much paler in colour and more brittle in appearance.

Glazes. The first glazes used by the Leeds Pottery were a soft, clear yellow, not the bright lemon-yellow of Cockpit Hill nor the yellowish-green of Wedgwood. Sometimes the Leeds glaze showed as a rich daffodil or buttercup yellow and sometimes tended towards a soft brown. Very occasionally a tendency to green occurs before 1775, but this is exceptional and almost certainly an accidental effect, the glaze having caught up some extraneous pigment or other glaze. The Leeds glazing was not generally so consistently uniform as the Wedgwood

---

(1) *Plate* 27A.

16

B. *Teapot. Height 4¾ in. Leeds. Circa 1775.*
Donald Towner. See page 19

and although most of the Leeds creamware was uncrazed there was always a tendency for the glaze to craze where it ran thickly; when this occurred the mesh so formed was usually fairly regular and about one-eighth inch square. From about the year 1775 the Leeds glaze differed from the Wedgwood and most other Staffordshire glazes in being primrose yellow in colour, though John Turner of Lane End, Staffordshire, used a very similar glaze at one time. Ware which received a full glaze appears very rich and creamy and is smooth to the touch. On the other hand, pieces which were more thinly glazed appear to be dry and chalky and feel somewhat rough. About 1780, a very soft greyish-green glaze was introduced. This was a much softer green than that used by Wedgwood, but very similar to a glaze used by the Yorkshire factory of Castleford. The glaze used by the Leeds Pottery on the elaborately-pierced chestnut baskets (1) and some other ware at this time was grey, sometimes tending towards green and occasionally towards blue. About 1780, an almost white body was introduced which has little to recommend it. About 1790 the Leeds Pottery introduced a blue tinted glaze for the so-called 'Pearlware'. The colour was a deep soft blue with no suggestion of green, differing in this respect from the pearlware of Wedgwood and other Staffordshire factories. Although it was usual in Pearlware to use only just sufficient blue to counteract the cream colour, the Leeds blue was so deep in colour as to give the ware a decidedly bluish cast. This was the glaze used on most of the Leeds square-based figures. About 1800 a bright pale-green glaze was used for a few years only, and about 1820 a straw-coloured glaze was introduced for a rich buff-coloured ware very different from the early deep cream colour.

Forms and Details. The early Leeds creamware, that is to say, the deep cream-coloured ware made before the year 1775, consisted very largely of teapots, coffee-pots, punch-pots, jugs and mugs. Tea-services as such do not appear to have been made at this time. Even at a much later date, tea- coffee- or chocolate-cups seem to have been made in small quantities only and to order. Perhaps this may account for the extreme scarcity of early creamware cups and saucers today. Punch-pots in the form of large teapots seem to have been in general use, some bearing the inscription 'Punch' painted upon them (2). The earliest teapots were small and globular, following the saltglaze forms with crabstock handle and spout (3), and having a small mushroom-shaped knob with a slight finial. Coffee-pots were pear-shaped, and both these and jugs had flat loop handles with pinched ends (4); but the saltglaze forms were soon discarded and new ones invented for the

(1) *Plate* 51A; (2) *Plate* 18B; (3) *Plate* 14A; (4) *Plate* 16.

creamware, though the globular shape for teapots always seems to have been favoured by the Leeds Pottery. There were many variations of this, but instances of the Wedgwood form, with rather flattened sides and top (1), having been made at the Leeds Pottery, are rare. The Leeds globular teapots are referred to in the drawing books as 'round' whereas the straight sided ones are referred to as 'square'. 'Engine-turned' decoration is used occasionally, and fluted tea or coffee-pots seem to be a special feature of the Leeds Pottery (2), being illustrated in the pattern books.

Much of the early Leeds creamware has a typical border-pattern of a diagonally set 'bead-and-reel' moulded in relief (3). This was superseded by the 'pearl' beading which came into use about 1775 (4). The handles, spouts, knobs and other details are discussed and illustrated in Appendix I (see page 64).

Enamelling. The following advertisement is from the *Leeds Intelligencer* for October 28th, 1760.

'Robinson and Rhodes, opposite the George, in Briggate, (Leeds), Enamel and Burn in Gold and Colour, Foreign and English China, and match broken setts of Enamel'd or Burnt-in China and Tea Ware and make them complete to any pattern required—either Indian or Dresden. They also enamel Coats of Arms, etc: and sell a good assortment of Foreign China and a great variety of useful English China of the newest improvement, which they will engage to wear as well as Foreign, and will change gratis if broke with hot water. They likewise enamel Stoneware which they sell as cheap as in Staffordshire. The best prices for Broken Flint Glass.'

It should be remembered that the word 'China' at this time was used to denote either porcelain or earthenware. The 'Stoneware' mentioned was fine white saltglaze (5). It was this firm that was responsible for most of the early enamelling, not only on the Leeds saltglaze and creamware but on the Wedgwood creamware as well (see page 35). David Rhodes was the senior partner. In 1763 Jasper Robinson gave up his partnership and was employed by Rhodes in the firm, which then became 'D. Rhodes & Co.'. In 1768 Rhodes left for London, taking with him an apprentice and another hand, and settled in St. Martin's Lane to work for Wedgwood as master enameller, until his own death in 1777 (see page 36). After 1768, the firm at Leeds may have continued under a new name and ownership (Rhodes retained the name 'D. Rhodes & Co.' while at St. Martin's Lane). But more probably the Leeds Pottery did their own enamelling from this

---

(1) *Plate* 79B; (2) *Plate* 15A; (3) *Plates* 19A, 26A, B; (4) *Plate* 36; (5) *Plates* 12, 13A, 30.

C. *Boxes with screw tops. Diam. 3 in. Leeds. Circa 1775.*
Donald Towner. See page 19

time, employing some of Rhodes' former enamellers, since enamelling in much the same style as before is found on some Leeds ware decorated after 1768, alongside the new styles of decoration then introduced. The enamelling was freely executed showing a fine vigour and stylization. At first the Leeds enamelling chiefly consisted of decoration in red and black only. Subjects which were most usual in these colours consisted of stylized flowers (1), birds (2), and landscapes, usually with a crossed tree, and houses with very black smoke coming from the chimneys (3). A gate was often introduced, as well as small clouds and birds. Figures, reminiscent of some saltglaze enamelling, either in red and black or in red only, were usual (4), as well as inscriptions within a freely-painted cartouche, in a fine convention (5). Another early style of painting which was done by Rhodes at Leeds consisted of flower-painting in which a thick pink enamel was used with other colours such as red, green, yellow and blue, as well as some in red and black only, the leaves often ending in a corkscrew-like shape. At a slightly later date, Rhodes, while still at Leeds, introduced a rosy purple which made a delightful and surprising clash with the bright orange-red which was such a feature of enamelling on creamware in general. Bands and stripes of these colours, sometimes with the addition of yellow and green, formed some original and good decoration (6). After Rhodes left Leeds, figures and stylized flowers in red monochrome remained a feature of Leeds enamelling, as well as the banded type of decoration and landscapes in brilliant colours, which often included a building with an oversize weathercock. Some good painting in underglaze blue was also done (7). Besides the enamelling found on tea and dessert ware, mention must be made of some particularly good enamelling on screw-top boxes, probably made for pomade (8). Snuff-boxes, some of which were in the form of heads, were also enamelled and are an interesting class of creamware (9). Leeds creamware, particularly plates, are often found with Dutch enamelling. The Dutch enamelling has a much drier look than the English; conspicuous on most of it is a purplish-brown colour. Dutch decorated plates with paintings of the Virgin and Child were sold to pilgrims visiting Kevelaar, as souvenirs. (The illustrated example (10) is by Turner of Lane End, Staffordshire.) Border patterns enamelled in the style of Wedgwood's Chelsea painted creamware, first appeared at Leeds about the year 1795 (11).

Creamware decorated with underglaze colours. In the past this type

---

(1) *Plate* 15B; (2) *Frontispiece*; (3) *Plate* 20; (4) *Plate* 14A; (5) *Plates* 17, 21; (6) *Colour Plate* B; (7) *Plate* 51B; (8) *Colour Plate* C; (9) *Plate* 41A; (10) *Plate* 96A; (11) *Plate* 68.

of ware has been closely associated with the name of Thomas Whieldon; but it is now certain that it was made at Derby, Liverpool, Leeds and Swinton, as well as in Stafforsdhire, where it was made by Whieldon, Wedgwood and others. Quite a considerable proportion of this type of ware has unmistakable Leeds characteristics. Teapots with the particular forms of double intertwined handles used at Leeds are not infrequent, though some of this type may have been made at Swinton, which was closely associated with the Leeds Pottery for a time.

Figures and animals with this form of decoration were made at Leeds (see page 22). Much Leeds tortoiseshell-ware has a dappled appearance (1), and a considerable amount of plain cream colour is often visible, especially on the underside of the object. The colours used were grass-green, a brown which often tended towards pink or crimson, yellow, plum, and a grey which sometimes tended towards purple or green. The pots usually possess the usual Leeds characteristics of handles, spouts, knobs and details of mouldings (see Appendix I). If the tortoiseshell coffee-pot illustrated (2) be compared with those shown on Plates 36 and 37, it will be noticed that the tortoiseshell coffee-pot embodies the main characteristics of form and detail of both the other two. Another type of creamware is decorated with vertical stripes of underglaze green (3). It is claimed that this type of ware was made in Staffordshire, which is probable, but the fact remains that most of the ware of this type with which one is conversant is undoubtedly of Leeds origin. Both this class of ware and another which consists of reeded bands filled in with the green glaze are referred to and illustrated in a Leeds drawing book, and specimens marked Leeds Pottery are also known.

Transfer-printing. It is uncertain when transfer-printing was first introduced at Leeds, but there is no doubt that decoration of this kind was done on a considerable scale at Leeds from about the year 1780. L. Jewitt, in *Ceramic Art of Great Britain* refers to the state of the Leeds Pottery in 1791, as follows; 'So great had the concern become that the yearly balance then struck amounted to over £51,500 and it is worth recording that in that year the value of the copper plates from which the transfer-printing was effected was £204.'

Of the colours used in the Leeds printing, the red was more orange in colour than in most of the prints by Sadler and Green on Wedgwood creamware. A purplish-black seems to have been peculiar to Leeds, and was often associated with a greenish-grey glaze which was sometimes crazed. The Victoria and Albert Museum coffee-pot,

---

(1) *Plate* 39; (2) *Plate* 38; (3) *Plate* 52A, B; (4) *Plate* 61; (5) *Plate* 62B.

marked 'Leeds Pottery' in the print, is in this colour (4). Printing in jet black occurs on Leeds creamware from an early date. The punch-kettle illustrated (5) is a very fine example. Less pleasing is printing in black on an almost white ground from about 1780. From about 1778, the black printing was sometimes washed over in enamel colours. Printing in sepia occurs in pieces of the early deep cream-coloured ware. At Leeds printing in underglaze blue was first introduced about 1815.

The subjects of Leeds transfer-printing are often similar to those used by Sadler and Green of Liverpool and were no doubt engraved from the same original sources. Amongst subjects which bear the Leeds Pottery mark in the transfer are the following:

1 and 2. 'The Chariot of Love' (I). There are two versions of this subject which sometimes occur on pieces which also bear the Leeds Pottery impressed mark.

3 and 4. Bull-fighting scenes are printed in black on a coffee-pot in the Yorkshire Museum, which was probably intended for export to Spain.

5. 'The Rev. John Wesley.'[1] The Leeds version of this subject differs from that which is sometimes signed Green Liverpool (2).

6. 'Love and obedience.'[1]

7. 'Faith.' These last three were probably printed for the Methodist Conferences held at Leeds in 1780.

8. 'The Vicar and Moses' printed in jet black and washed over in enamel colours occurs on a jug in the Yorkshire Museum. The arms of Leeds, the golden fleece, are enamelled in front, also 'J.B.' and 'S.B.' above the words 'Success to the Leeds Manufactory'. The initials J.B. and S.B. probably refer to John Barwick, who was one of the partners of the Leeds Pottery in 1781, and his wife.[2]

9. 'Arms of the Moderns' (Masonic) (3).

For notes on creamware printed in black with scenes from the story of the Prodigal Son, etc., see pages 30–32.

Pierced Decoration. An enormous amount of plain useful cream-ware was made at the Leeds Pottery. This is generally of fine form but not so light in weight as the more delicate pieces, as it was made considerably thicker in order to stand up to more general usage. The lists published with the Leeds Pattern Books[3] give an idea of the extra-

[1] Illustrated in, Donald C. Towner, *Handbook of Leeds Pottery*, Leeds, 1951, p. 44.

[2] Illustrated in, O. Grabham, *Yorkshire Potteries, Pots and Potters*, York, 1916, p. 58; and in A. Hurst, *Catalogue of the Boynton Collection*, York, 1922, p. 62.

[3] These lists, of which the originals are very rare, were reproduced by J. and F. Kidson in *Historical Notices of the Leeds Old Pottery*, Leeds, 1892, pp. 33–44.

(I) *Plate* 61; (2) *Plate* 83B; (3) *Plate* 60.

ordinary variety of utilitarian creamware made. The wares, however, for which the Leeds Pottery is particularly famed are creamware with pierced openwork decoration (1) and the elaborate centre-pieces (2). These last were an extraordinary feat of technical achievement. Chestnut-baskets with elaborately pierced sides and cover are sometimes marked 'LEEDS * POTTERY' or 'HARTLEY GREENS & CO.' (see Appendix III). Twig baskets and dishes of basket-work pattern, were made in quantities for dessert; these were somewhat similar to those made by other factories though many made at Leeds were characterized by having a plain centre (3).

Figures. It is not usually realized that the Leeds Pottery produced figures decorated with coloured glazes in the style that is so much associated with the name of Thomas Whieldon, but such is the case. A group in the Victoria and Albert Museum (4) in this type of colouring is further decorated by the application of eleven flowers from a single mould; these flowers being the upper portion of the particular form of flower-knob used by the Leeds Pottery for teapots (see Appendix I, Plate V, fig. 4c). The style of head-dress worn by the lady in this group was first introduced about 1770. The date of this piece could therefore be placed a few years later. A very similar group, but without the applied flowers, in the Willett Collection at Brighton, is in saltglaze. The slight differences of costume suggest that the saltglaze group was made about 1760. A figure sometimes called 'Prince Rupert'[1] (5) is decorated with the same applied floral motifs that occur on other pieces of Leeds Pottery.

Animals and birds were also made at Leeds, some of them being decorated with a soft grass-green glaze often with additional touches of grey or yellow (6). A number of figures and animals, however, were also made in the same brilliant rich creamware but were left uncoloured. The best Leeds figures both of this type and that which succeeded it, namely the square base figures, are very pleasing. The modeller for the most part chose very intimate homely subjects and endowed them with character. Most of the female figures seem to represent the same young woman, who though slightly snub-nosed has great charm (7). The classical figures though good are rather less interesting. Unfortunately one or two of the old moulds survived the factory, and figures have been made from these in modern times and impressed 'LEEDS .

[1] The names 'Hamlet' and 'Ophelia' have also been given to this figure and its companion with more seeming justification. A creamware figure of 'Ophelia' painted in enamel colours is also known.

(1) *Plates* 43, 51A; (2) *Plates* 48, 49; (3) *Plate* 42B; (4) *Plate* 54; (5) *Plate* 55; (6) *Plate* 53A, B; (7) *Plate* 56.

POTTERY'. Such figures are more grey in appearance and the glaze on them is usually crazed. The brilliance of the original creamware never seems to have been successfully imitated.

Certain characteristics may be noted in attempting to identify the Leeds figures. The figures are completely open underneath (that is to say that on turning the piece upside-down, one can see the whole of the interior). The only exceptions to this rule are the few copies made at Leeds of figures which originated at other factories. Most of the figures with square bases are of 'pearlware', with an extremely smooth and brilliant heavy blue glaze, free from any tinge of green. This glaze often gives the figures a distinct bluish cast. The base itself is deeper than that of the Staffordshire 'square-base' figures, and a nick is often discernible inside the corners. This was deliberately made with a pointed tool to prevent the development of fire-cracks. The enamel colours include a clear sea-green, orange, pinkish-mauve, pale yellow and black. Full use was made of spots as a form of enamel decoration.

The following is a short list of some of the Leeds figures which are known to have been marked with the original Leeds Pottery impressed mark:

1–4	The Seasons[1]	13	Venus
5	Skater	14	Neptune (13, 14 a pair)
6–7	Falconers (1)	15	Bacchus
8	Boy with a Dog	16	Air (3)
9–10	Pair of Musicians[1]	17	Water[2] (16, 17 a pair)
11	Sir Isaac Newton	18	Minerva
12	Andromache (2)	19	Mars.[1]

Late Wares. During the early years of the nineteenth century many new types of ware were introduced by the Leeds Pottery. About 1800 a creamware that had a slightly grey appearance and was very light in weight was made. It was decorated with formal designs and sprigs in underglaze mineral colours of brown, deep blue, sage-green and orange-buff. This class of ware is usually associated with Pratt of Fenton, but was also made at Bristol and elsewhere. Black basalt ware was also first introduced at the Leeds Pottery about 1800. By about 1810 the Leeds Pottery, in common with a number of others, was

[1] Illustrated in, Donald C. Towner, *Handbook of Leeds Pottery*, Leeds, 1951, p. 42.
[2] Illustrated in, Bernard Rackham, *Catalogue of the Schreiber Collection*, Vol. II. (Victoria and Albert Museum), London, 1930, Plate 50.

(1) *Plates* 56, 57; (2) *Plate* 58; (3) *Plate* 59.

producing marbled creamware in tones of black, brown, brownish-red and cream. Leeds examples of this ware as well as of a buff-coloured ware frequently consisted of mugs decorated with moulded swags and portrait medallions of Admiral Keppel, Lord Nelson and others. After 1810, the Leeds Pottery added to its production numerous types of simple band and check patterns. These included vertical bands of black or dark brown, small chequered patterns in black or pale blue, and broad horizontal bands of orange-buff, the contrasting colour in each case being cream. In addition creamware with enamelled formal border patterns in the style of Wedgwood was produced (1), as well as dessert services painted with named flowers copied from illustrations in botanical books, lustre-ware (chiefly silver), and a very deep buff-coloured ware decorated with monochrome painted landscapes or with holly and ivy leaves in dark green.

A number of figures of horses about 16 inches high, said to have been made for display in the windows of harness makers' and corn chandlers' shops, were made in the vicinity of Leeds soon after 1800. These are inferior in both body and glaze, to the creamware of the Leeds Pottery. And although a horse of this kind in the Yorkshire Museum has the letters L.P. enamelled on a corner of the saddle cloth, others have the impressed mark 'LEEDS-POTTERY' in compressed letters, which was not the mark of the original Leeds Pottery, but might have been that of one of the several smaller creamware factories working at Leeds about 1800. It is probable that marks in close imitation of those of the original Leeds Pottery were deliberately used by these factories in the hope that their productions would be mistaken for those of the larger and more famous pottery. But generally speaking all these late wares are of little ceramic interest in comparison with the fine products of the Leeds Pottery made during the eighteenth century.

There has been a great deal of uncertainty regarding the origin of a large group of creamware teapots made about 1780, either painted in enamels with subjects such as 'Aurora' (2) or transfer-printed in black and enamelled over with such subjects as 'The Prodigal Son' (3). There is no doubt that many of these teapots were made at Leeds, but the whole group is discussed in Chapter 5 under 'William Greatbatch', pages 30–32.

The Pattern and Drawing Books. Pattern books were issued by a number of leading potteries in England. They were catalogues with engraved illustrations and descriptive lists of the wares in current production for the guidance of wholesale or retail traders in England

---

(1) *Plate* 68; (2) *Plate* 64; (3) *Plate* 66A.

or abroad in placing their orders. The Leeds Pottery first published a pattern book in 1783. Books of working drawings for use in the Leeds Pottery itself have been preserved. Three of these are at the Victoria and Albert Museum and nine others at the Leeds City Art Gallery. Both these and the pattern books are discussed in Appendix III, page 79.

Marks. A very small proportion of the Leeds creamware was marked. It is possible that the Leeds Pottery only marked those pieces which were destined for other factories for resale. A frequently repeated note in the Leeds order books is as follows: 'Ordered at Swinton, to be marked etc.' (see Appendix II, Plate III). The most usual Leeds Pottery mark consists of the words 'LEEDS * POTTERY' in capital letters, impressed, with an asterisk between the two words. Unfortunately this mark has been used on creamware of recent manufacture which has caused a great deal of confusion amongst those who are not intimate with the original creamware of the Leeds Pottery. Not only are modern pieces which bear the Leeds Pottery mark often bought in the belief that they are the products of the original factory, but collectors and others who have been disillusioned in this respect, often refuse to buy original Leeds creamware because it is marked and therefore likely to be modern.

For illustrations of the Leeds Pottery marks with notes, see Appendix III.

After the bankruptcy of the Leeds Pottery in 1820, the factory continued to be worked by a number of successive proprietors, whose names and dates of occupancy are as follows:

1825–37	Samuel Wainwright.
1837–41	Leeds Pottery Company.
1841–49	Stephen and John Chappell.
1853–61	Warburton and Britton.
1861–72	Richard Britton.
1872–78	Richard Britton & Sons,

after which Messrs. Taylor had it for a few years. At first an attempt was made to continue with the creamware, but the composition of body and glaze was altered. Warburton and Britton made some elaborate and ornate vases. A pair of jars, made by Warburton and Britton about 1857 are at the Yorkshire Museum, York.[1] In 1892 when Joseph and Frank Kidson published their book, *Leeds Old Pottery*, the factory was untenanted and fast becoming a ruin. Today in 1957, nothing remains.

[1] These jars are illustrated in Donald C. Towner, *Handbook of Leeds Pottery*, Leeds, 1951, p. 47.

5

WILLIAM GREATBATCH

William Greatbatch was apprentice and afterwards modeller to Thomas Whieldon at Fenton, Staffordshire. When the Whieldon-Wedgwood partnership was dissolved in 1759, Greatbatch left Whieldon and began work at Lower Lane, Fenton, under an agreement to supply his wares to Josiah Wedgwood. It becomes evident from the correspondence between the two men that Wedgwood realized the inventive genius of Greatbatch and looked to him for wares of novel and ingenious designs until such time as his own position was secured by the success of his creamware. The wares made by Greatbatch, which were of a common earthenware body as well as some of a fine creamware, were delivered to Wedgwood in the biscuit state ready to be glazed. Greatbatch moved to Lane Delph in 1764, and the following letter seems to mean that he supplied ware to Wedgwood similar to that made by Whieldon.

'Lane Delph, May 1764. To Mr. Josiah Wedgwood. There are ready two of the crates of Pine Apple ware and a large quantity of plates about a gross & 1–2 of light colour teapots and a good quantity of China tpts. the same as Mr. Whieldon & other sorts.'

By 'China tpts.' he undoubtedly refers to teapots, usually hexagonal, with Chinese motifs in relief. Greatbatch seems to use the words 'China' and 'Chinese' indiscriminately. Teapots of this kind were usually of a somewhat coarse earthenware decorated with clouded underglaze colours; some rare examples exist, however, which are of a fine quality creamware painted in enamel colours. It is tempting to think that the two following letters have a direct reference to the two teapots of this type illustrated (1).[1]

[1] It may be argued that this suggestion is impossible in view of the fact that the 'widow' knob was modelled from Dame Sneyd who posed for it in 1774 and that the lap-dog was modelled for Wedgwood by P. Stephan in the same year. It must be pointed out, however, that there were at least four versions of the 'widow' and several of the lap-dog. The original versions were undoubtedly modelled by W. Greatbatch soon after 1760 as these occur on some early cauliflower-ware tea- and

(1) *Plate* 71A, B.

'Lower Lane, Dec. 9th. 1763.

I have sent you a square China Teapot as a specimen, should be glad to have your judgment on it the couler is light I own but dare ingage to make any quantity of a darker Couler if required. Wm. Greatbatch.'

'Dec. 12th. 1763.

I have received yours wrote by Mr. Byerley and have made a new handle and spout to the China Teapot. Wm. Greatbatch.'

A saltglaze mould for teapots or tea-caddies of this description is illustrated (1).

The following bill will give an idea of the variety of wares Greatbatch supplied to Wedgwood.

'July 22nd. 1760.

3 Foxglove teapts.[1]	12s.
2 Large Leaves	
7 Pr. Cornu Copias	
3 Pr. Large fluted Candlesticks	
2 Melon sauce Bts & stds.	
2 Leaf candlesticks	
2 fluted tpts.	
2 Mossaic Do.	
2 Woodbine do.	
4 Green do.	
2 Chinese do.	
5 Doz Large Toys	

Left at the Cross Keys Wood Street
London.'

In addition to these patterns, some of which are quite unknown to us today, it is apparent from the correspondence that Greatbatch also supplied Wedgwood with ware in the form of cauliflowers, pineapples,

coffee-pots of his make. (Besides the four versions of the Wedgwood 'widow' knob, there were many other versions on the wares of other potters.) The first 'widow' knob is the young woman wrapped in a shawl and wearing a bonnet, which occurs on the two teapots in question. The second version is a girl wearing a shawl and a flat brimmed hat which is not covered by the shawl. A third version is of an older woman with arms folded. She is completely wrapped in a shawl which covers her head like a cowl. The fourth is of a younger woman, who is wearing a coif, which is not entirely covered by the shawl. It is probable that the third or fourth versions, which also vary in posture from the first two, represent Dame Sneyd. The dog varies considerably both in type and posture.

[1] Saltglaze moulds for 'foxglove' and 'Chinese' pattern teapots are in the Wedgwood Museum, Barlaston.

(1) *Plate 70.*

apples, pears, quinces and other fruits. Green teapots mentioned in the bill may refer to teapots to be coloured green rather than those already glazed and were, no doubt, the well-known teapots entirely covered on the outside with a fine deep green glaze, the inside sometimes dis-closing a fine quality creamware.[1] Gilding was frequently added. There is a tradition that Greatbatch modelled the saltglaze wall-vases in the form of a cornucopia with a bust of 'Flora' in relief (I), [2] and this seems to be well borne out by facts, though somewhat similar wall-vases were made at Leeds. A saltglaze mould taken from the Leeds Pottery is illustrated (2). Four female figures occur on cream-ware wall-vases of this type, denoting the Seasons. A four-sided tea-caddy made from the same mould as the 'Flora' wall-vase is of probable Greatbatch origin (3). This has the same rich cream glaze as the two hexagonal teapots already referred to, which is quite distinct from the greenish glazes of Wedgwood.

A pattern for which Greatbatch was partly responsible was the 'shell', which was used so much by Wedgwood and copied by others. A creamware shell-pattern spout was excavated at Fenton Low and is now in the Castle Museum, Norwich. The same spout also occurs on an enamelled teapot in the author's collection (4) and on a beautiful, deep green teapot in the Glaisher collection, Cambridge, as well as on teapots of Leeds manufacture, some of which bear that pottery's im-pressed mark (see Appendix I, Plate II, fig. 3). The following letter however, probably, refers to a more elaborate type of shell pattern which occurs on some of Wedgwood's creamware (5) (see Appendix I, Plate II, fig. 2).

'Sir,

Desire you'll send six guineas by the Bearer hereof and you'll greatly oblige your humble servant.

Wm. Greatbatch.

P.S. I expected your advice in the shape of the Teapots agreed on. The work is complicated for the shell and other teapot. Should be glad you would cut the shape upon paper you would have them to be and whether you would have a ground upon them or not.

Saturday noon   Lower Lane,
To Mr. Josiah Wedgwood, Burslem.'

The correspondence also shows that Greatbatch bought small quanti-

---

[1] In 1763 Wedgwood was obtaining copper scales to form this green glaze from Robinson & Rhodes of Leeds, see p. 36.
[2] A mould for these is at the Wedgwood Museum, Barlaston.

(I) *Plate 72*; (2) *Plate 45*; (3) *Plate 73*; (4) *Plate 77*A; (5) *Plate 85*.

ties of transfer-printed ware from Wedgwood for which he paid in cash.

'Lane Delf   Sept. 16. 1763.

Please to send by bearer a 2 dish Tpt. with the queen printed upon.'

The following letter is also of interest as evidence that Greatbatch modelled teapots in the shape of fruits for Wedgwood. These were afterwards decorated by Wedgwood in underglaze colours.

'Lower Lane   Friday noon.

Sir,

Please to send word by the Bearer whether we shou'd or not have sent you an apple Tpt. shou'd be glad to know if you wou'd have leaves on the side the same as use to be, send a Tpt with Earl Bute on it, have sent Cash to pay for it.'

The following letter to Wedgwood shows that ware to be enamelled was sent to a Mr. Courzen for that purpose.

'Lower Lane.   12 July 1763

Sir,

I shall send Mr. Courzen's ware to his painting shop to Night.

Wm. Greatbatch.'

It is not likely that Mr. Courzen had bought the ware from Greatbatch, as in that case it would have been a matter of very little interest to Wedgwood. As the ware would have to be glazed before being enamelled, this letter shows that some glazing, at any rate, was done by Greatbatch at Lower Lane. The two teapots in Chinese style may be examples of creamware enamelled by Courzen (1).

Greatbatch continued to work for Wedgwood at Lane Delph for some time. According to a letter written by Thomas Byerley to Josiah Wedgwood the second, Greatbatch later worked for John Turner of Lane End, but the dates of his employment there are not known.

The following two entries are from the *London Gazette.*

'Feb. 1782

Bankrupt—William Greatbatch, potter,
                Stoke-on-Trent.'

'26 April 1788

Bankrupt—William Greatbatch, potter,
                Stoke.'

In 1788 he went to ask for assistance at Etruria where it would seem he was employed in receipting the deliveries of clay to the factory.

---

(1) *Plate* 71A, B.

Dr. Simeon Shaw on page 190 of his *History of the Staffordshire Potteries* published in 1829 writes:

'Another excellent modeller, in fact a general workman of first rate abilities, was Mr. William Greatbatch sometime employed by Messrs. Whieldon and Wedgwood and had commenced business on his own account at the manufactory at Fenton, now a small part of Bourne, Baker & Bourne where he produced numerous articles of improved patterns and kinds and for some time had a rapid sale of teapots on which was printed in black by Thomas Radford the history of the 'Prodigal Son' but heavy losses at length ruined him. Mr. Wedgwood aware of the talents of his former servant engaged him for life at the very high wages of five shillings a day whether at work or play, and a house rent free which sum was regularly paid him till his death, though he survived his master.'

The teapots mentioned in this statement of Simeon Shaw's form part of a very large group of creamware, a number of typical examples from which are illustrated (1). Some of the teapots in this group have the following inscription printed upon them, 'Published as the Act directs Jany. 4 1778 by W. Greatbatch Lane-Delf Staffordshire' (2) (Appendix III, Mark 39), while on others in the same group, the name 'Greatbatch', only, appears as part of the engraving. The inscription 'Published as the Act directs' followed by the date and a name, was frequently inscribed at the foot of engravings. The name refers to that of the publisher, but sometimes the engraver and the publisher were one and the same person. A single name by itself in an engraving usually denotes the engraver, though the printer's name or the name of the factory sometimes occur, but in such cases, these are usually placed a little apart from the engraving itself. Thomas Radford, referred to in Simeon Shaw's statement, worked as an engraver at Cockpit Hill, Derby, probably till it closed down in 1779. If one compares Radford's signed engravings on Derby creamware with those of the 'Prodigal Son' series, which are clearly all by one hand, a considerable difference of style and technique will be apparent. It would seem therefore, that Simeon Shaw's statement that the 'Prodigal Son' series was 'printed in black by Thomas Radford' cannot easily be accepted as meaning that the series was engraved by him. Jewitt, it is true, mentions as made by Greatbatch, a mug with a print of 'The World in Planisphere' signed by Radford.[1] Mugs with this subject

[1] Creamware mugs and jugs bearing the title 'The World in Planisphere' but printed in colour and unsigned are probably of Bristol origin (3).

(1) *Plate* 65A, B; 66A, B; 67A, B; 82B; (2) *Plate* 66B; (3) *Plate* 96B.

printed in black and signed by Radford are known. The print on such mugs is left uncoloured and corresponds much more closely in style with Radford's work at Derby, but the mugs themselves are of biscuit-ware, and should almost certainly be assigned to Baddeley of Shelton, who is known to have made this type of ware. This attribution receives support from the fact, reported by Chaffers, that Thomas Radford's name appears in the 1802 list of persons connected with the pottery trade, where he was then working for J. Baddeley.

As the 'Prodigal Son' engravings can hardly be by Radford, we have no alternative to accepting the evidence of the signature that they were engraved by William Greatbatch himself. It may seem surprising that a modeller should take to engraving, but it will be seen that the engravings themselves are not the work of a competent professional engraver. Though the Greatbatch family was a large one and a number of descendants from it became engravers at a later date, no other engraver of this name is known to have been working about the year 1778.[1]

If the teapots themselves be examined it will be noticed that they are not entirely of one manufacture. This precludes William Greatbatch from having made them all. A transfer-printed teapot of this group, which is at the Victoria and Albert Museum, is of Wedgwood manufacture (1) and there is strong circumstantial evidence that most of the others were made at Leeds. Two explanations are possible. Either William Greatbatch bought teapots in the white from Leeds and elsewhere, and printed his own engravings upon them; or his copper-plates were sold, perhaps after his bankruptcy, and came into the possession of Wedgwood, Leeds, and perhaps other factories. It is worth recording that the first two subjects in the 'Prodigal Son' series appear in alternative versions—perhaps the beginning of a second series never completed—on teapots of uncertain origin (2). The engraved 'Aurora' subject also served as inspiration for a version painted solely in enamel colours, on creamware teapots undoubtedly made at Leeds (3).

The following is a list of some of the subjects engraved by William Greatbatch which occur on creamware teapots.

1. 'The Prodigal Son receives his patrimony.'
2. 'The Prodigal Son taking his leave.'
3. 'The Prodigal Son in excess' (4).
4. 'The Prodigal Son in misery.'

[1] A William Greatbatch and H. Greatbatch exhibited engravings at the Royal Academy in the early part of the nineteenth century.

(1) *Plate* 82B; (2) *Plate* 67B; (3) *Plate* 64A; (4) *Plate* 66A.

5. 'The Prodigal Son returns reclaimed.'
6. 'The Prodigal Son feasted on his return.'
7. 'The Prodigal Son receives his patrimony.' 2nd series (1).
8. 'The Prodigal Son taking his leave.' 2nd series.
9. 'The Fortune Teller.'
10. 'Juno.'
11. 'Aurora' (Two versions) (2).
12. 'Captain Cook being directed by Brittania' (3).
13. 'Admiral Keppel' (4).
14. 'Man of War in full sail.'
15. 'A Lady and Gentleman walking in a garden.'
16. 'Harlequin and columbine discovered in an arbour.'
17. 'Twelve Houses of Heaven' (5).
18. 'The world, with sun, moon and stars.'
19. 'Cybele.'

---

(1) *Plate* 67B; (2) *Plate* 65A, 82B; (3) *Plate* 67A; (4) *Plate* 65B; (5) *Plate* 66B.

6

JOSIAH WEDGWOOD

It has already been shown that a fine creamware had been in existence a considerable number of years before Wedgwood severed his partnership with Whieldon in 1759 and started on his own account, first at the 'Ivy House' Burslem, and then in 1764 at the 'Brick House' Burslem, known later as the 'Bell Works'. The manufacture of Wedgwood's creamware probably dates from 1760 or the early part of 1761, although some experimental pieces had doubtless been made during the five years that Wedgwood was in partnership with Whieldon at Fenton Hall. During this period and for a number of years after, he produced some very fine creamware decorated with clouded underglaze colours (tortoiseshell ware), some examples of which are marked 'Wedgwood'.

The first known examples of Wedgwood's creamware are of a rich buff colour covered with a greenish glaze which was inclined to craze, and there is no doubt that Wedgwood's chief efforts at this time were directed towards developing a creamware which would not only be more refined in body, glaze, design and finish, but would also be paler in colour. At first the body was improved by the use of clays from Dorset and Devonshire which also made refinements of potting possible, and by 1763 the creamware was already much paler in colour. On first leaving Whieldon, Wedgwood had entered into an arrangement whereby William Greatbatch was to supply him with teapots for glazing (see page 26); and some fine creamware teapots covered with a deep green glaze on the outside are of this period, as well as teapots in the form of fruits and vegetables, such as the melon and cauliflower. Between 1763 and 1767 Wedgwood made a great many changes both in the body and glaze and also in the methods of manufacture. Eliza Meteyard in her *Life of Wedgwood* tells how Wedgwood improved the kilns as well as every tool, instrument and apparatus at the factory, sometimes replacing them with new types of his own invention. The most important change, however, as already stated in the Introduction, was the incorporation of Cornish china-clay and stone into both body and glaze. This not only produced a much paler creamware but also gave it a lightness and brilliance which was wholly new.

The following letter written by Wedgwood in 1768 to his London office shows that having abandoned the deep cream colour he was not in a position to resort to it again, at this time at any rate.

'With respect to the colour of my ware, I endeavour to make it as pale as possible to continue it cream-colour and find my customers in general, though not every individual of them, think the alteration I have made in that respect a great improvement, but it is impossible that any one colour, even though it were to come down from Heaven, should please every taste, and I cannot regularly make two cream-colours, a deep and a light shade, without having two works for that purpose.' . . .

It follows that since Wedgwood in 1768 was unable to make both the deep and the pale coloured creamware at the same time, the smaller factories were still less able to do so. This fact is a valuable aid to the identification of early creamware. Thus the Wedgwood cream-ware of from 1763 to 1770 was much paler in colour than the Leeds of the corresponding period. It was also paler than the Daniels' cream-ware of 1773 as is evidenced by a cake basket in the British Museum with the incised signature and date 'John Daniel, 1773' (see Appendix III, Mark 101). But the Warburton creamware of this period was probably very similar to Wedgwood's (see page 9).

Glazes. The glaze on the earliest marked pieces of Wedgwood's creamware, as already stated, was strongly tinged with yellowish-green, and sometimes showed considerable crazing. With the refining of the body, however, a finer glaze was introduced which though also greenish, appeared much paler, as it was more thinly and evenly applied, with the consequent elimination of crazing. This was a glaze of great beauty which when applied to the creamware body seemed to glow with life. It was usually of sufficient strength of colour to give the ware a slight greenish tinge. This is particularly apparent on the inside of teapots, which are usually greener than those of Leeds manufacture. After about 1763 crazing on Wedgwood's creamware was rare. Except for some whitish creamware which was covered with a blue-green glaze and the pearlware which was coated with a sufficient quantity of bluish glaze to counteract the cream colour of the body, the creamware continued to be coated with the yellow-green glaze which though remaining the same tint became consistently paler till by the end of the century it was almost colourless. The blue glaze of Wedgwood's pearlware had a slightly greenish tinge which is entirely absent in the Leeds pearlware. Although Wedgwood invented the name 'pearlware', creamware with a bluish glaze was being produced in Staffordshire between 1740 and 1750 (1). Probably the most distinc-

---

(1) *Plates* 1, 2.

tive characteristic of the later Wedgwood glazes is their thin and even application, which tended to produce an almost mechanical uniformity of surface.

Forms and Details. Wedgwood, while preserving a globular form for his teapots, modified it by compressing the top and sides (1). This shape was used for the great majority of his creamware teapots throughout the eighteenth century, but was quickly copied by other potters. The adoption of Wedgwood forms by other Staffordshire potters was probably encouraged by Josiah himself, as he formed what he called 'banks'. These consisted of stocks of ware made by a number of other potters from which he could make up his crates when he himself was unable to meet all the orders for creamware which he received. This arrangement was mutual. Letters and bills from Anne Warburton and Sons, the Daniels and other potters, dating from 1762 to 1799 and now in the Wedgwood Museum, Barlaston, refer to ware sold to, or bought from, Josiah Wedgwood. A letter quoted by Miss Meteyard shows Josiah's annoyance at the inability of Thomas Byerley, Wedgwood's nephew and London representative, to distinguish between the Wedgwood creamware and that of the 'banks'.[1]

Enamelling. The first reference to any enamelling in the Wedgwood correspondence is contained in the letter quoted on page 29; written by William Greatbatch to Wedgwood on 12 July 1763 in which Mr. Courzen's painting shop is mentioned. It may be that the enamelling on teapots of the Chinese hexagonal pattern (2) was the work of Courzen. A letter[2] dated 11 March 1763, shows that Wedgwood had already entered into business negotiations with Robinson and Rhodes enamellers of Leeds (see page 18) who at that time were buying his ware and had supplied him with the name of an engraver to cut the seals or brass stamps for his applied ornaments; the following order is enclosed in this letter:

'1 doz. flowered 18ˢ[3] teapotts mellon colour
1 ,, 18ˢ do ½ doz. 24ˢ
1 ,, 24ˢ do.—pine apple shape.
4 green oval fruit basketts and Dishes the basketts about 7½ inches broad.
12 dry red teapotts some of them with Crab tree spouts.

[1] For further notes on the forms and details of Wedgwood's creamware see Appendix I.
[2] This and all other letters relating to Wedgwood and quoted in this book are from the Wedgwood correspondence at the Wedgwood Museum, Barlaston.
[3] 18ˢ, 24ˢ, etc., refer to sizes.

(1) *Plate* 79B; (2) *Plate* 71A, B.

1 doz. Teapotts, a few of them 24s of your neatest and newest
fashioned sort.

In sending the above mentioned soon you'll oblige us much and
we shall want many more of them.

for Partner and Self

Yr most humble Servt. Davd. Rhodes.'

On 2 May 1763 Rhodes was supplying Wedgwood with copper
scales for his green glaze.

The following letters to Wedgwood perhaps denote the beginning
of actual work by Rhodes on Wedgwood's creamware.

'Leeds 21st November. 1764.

'I received your Favour, and shall be glad to serve you in anything I
can do. I have burnt Gold on China often and am certain I can do it
on your ware; . . .

My partner has turned over the business to me since March last and
works for me at it.

Sr. Your most humble Servt.

Davd. Rhodes.'

'Leeds. Dec. 13. 1764.

Desire you would send me the Cream Coloured teapotts immediately if you have them.—

Davd. Rhodes.'

Unfortunately there are no further records of Rhodes till 24 March
1768 when Wedgwood wrote to Bentley telling him how he had
acquired the lease of a warehouse in St. Martin's Lane and continues
—'I have already agreed with one very useful Tenant A Master
Enameler and China piecer . . . I have long had connections with this
Man, who is sober and steady, he is just come out of Yorkshire to settle
here . . . he paints flowers and Landskips very prettily, prepares a
pretty good powder gold, and has a tolerable notion of Colours. He has
an Apprentice and another hand, I have set him to work upon Table
and desert ware, and shall get his rooms ready in St. Martin's Lane
immediately.' On 20 June 1768, Wedgwood writes to Mr. Cox,
Queen's Arms, London, as follows:

'I have yours today of ye 18 and have one from Mr Rhodes ac-
quainting me he has got a partner[1] who has Enam.d at Paris and does
it with great Elegance and wants to begin upon some small plates
immediately wch. you'l please to furnish them with I shall write to
Mr. Rhodes this post.

Yr. frd. and Sert. J.W.'

[1] David Rhodes entered into partnership with William Hopkins Craft. Receipts,
at the Wedgwood Museum, Barlaston, signed by Rhodes and Craft cover the years
1769 and 1770, after which the partnership was probably dissolved. Four signed and
dated examples of William Craft's enamelling on copper are at the British Museum.

Bills from Rhodes dating from Dec. 27th 1768 till Dec. 23rd 1769 amounting to £178.10.1. are headed 'Ware of Mr. Josiah Wedgwood to be enamelled at D. Rhodes & Co'.

There are numerous letters in the correspondence showing how highly Wedgwood esteemed Rhodes as an enameller.

'19 Nov. 1769. To Thos. Bentley
I have reserved my house at Burslem for Mr. Rhodes and his Men, it is quite ready for him and when he comes you shall have Mr. Bakewell, but we must have somebody here to vein and finish the vases—'

Types of painting mentioned in the letters as being done by Rhodes are: flowers, landscapes, figures, husks, table-plate with 'Purple and Gold', as well as veining (marbling) and painting on Etruscan Vases.

'To Thos. Bentley, Queen's Arms, Newport Street.
10 Jan. 1770
. . . If I had Mr. Rhodes here you shod. soon have some Etruscan Vases painted at Etruria, but I cannot attempt anything farther without such assistance . . . When does Mr. Rhodes intend to be here . . .
J. W.'

The teapot at the Victoria and Albert Museum having a figure in a landscape can be identified as the work of Rhodes (1). The treatment of details, such as the crossed tree and foliage,[1] is identical with Leeds saltglaze and creamware painting. On the reverse of this same teapot is some fine flower painting (2), also similar in treatment to some done at Leeds. (The cover to this teapot was made at the Leeds Pottery and is a replacement.) Some pieces of Wedgwood's creamware are enamelled in the same style, but show a different treatment of foliage and may therefore have been done by one of Rhodes' assistants.[2] This treatment of foliage occurs on a teapot in the Castle Museum, Norwich, which has a standing figure enamelled on one side and is inscribed 'Success to Sir Charles Holte Esq.' (3). Sir Charles Holte was a contestant at Birmingham for the parliamentary election of 1774, so that the teapot can be dated precisely.

In April 1773, Wedgwood writes,

'I think Mr. Rhodes cannot be better employ'd than in painting Landskips.' The teapot with a Landscape illustrated (4), may date from about this time.

[1] The 'hooked' treatment of foliage occurs on much of the early Leeds enamelling.
[2] It would appear that a single piece of decoration was often the work of more than one enameller.

(1) *Plate 76*A; (2) *Plate 78*B; (3) *Plate 77*B; (4) *Plate 76*B.

The colours used by Rhodes for figures, flowers and landscapes on Wedgwood creamware are red, black, green, rosy purple and yellow. During the time that Rhodes was at Leeds the palette he then used was mostly confined to red and black though he sometimes introduced touches of green, rosy purple, yellow and other colours.

Among other enamelled designs found on Wedgwood's creamware we may first mention the very delightful and original banded and diapered patterns (1). These also are painted in red, black, rosy purple, green and yellow, and occur not only on Wedgwood creamware but also on that of the Leeds Pottery. On some pieces, this type of decoration is combined with flower painting in the style of Rhodes. It therefore seems to be certain that he was their author.

A slightly different type of flower painting occurs on Wedgwood creamware, in which a thick opaque rosy pink is conspicuous, other colours used being red, green, blue, black and yellow (2). Very similar painting is also found on Leeds creamware, and there is little doubt that such enamelling is also by Rhodes. Teapots enamelled by Rhodes in all the above styles are sometimes found with rose-coloured handles and spouts. Wedgwood teapots with this style of painting are a deeper cream than the enamelled teapots already mentioned and are earlier in date. An enameller's mark of three green spots arranged in the form of a triangle sometimes occurs on teapots painted both in this and the banded style already mentioned (3).

Another type of flower painting somewhat similar to the last, but in which the rosy pink is replaced by a rosy purple (4), is less vigorous and of a slightly different technique, and the teapots on which it is found would appear to have been made after 1770. This enamelling may be by James Bakewell, who was mentioned in a letter from Josiah Wedgwood to Thos. Bentley dated 23rd May 1770:

'Bakewell has set his mind to be a good enamel Painter and really improves much both in flowers and in Copying figures.'

Some freely-painted naturalistic flowers in purple or crimson monochrome occur on dessert services, whose borders usually have a fringe or 'feathered' edging of the same colour (5). They are sometimes marked underneath in enamel with the letters 'B', 'D' or 'G', which probably stand for James Bakewell, Thomas Dimcock and Thomas Green, whose names appear on a Wedgwood account for enamelling dated October 1770. Painting of a similar nature was done in black and yellow (6). This and the purple enamelling marked with the letter 'B' were undoubtedly painted by Bakewell, as the following letter shows.

(1) *Plates* 80A, B, 81; (2) *Plate* 79A; (3) *Plate* 80A; (4) *Plate* 79B; (5) *Plate* 86A; (6) *Plate* 86B.

D. *Mug. Height 5 in. Wedgwood. Circa 1770.*
Painted by D. Rhodes.
Donald Towner. See pages 57, 58

'22 July, 1770   Josiah Wedgwood to Thos. Bentley.
. . . If Mr. Rhodes stays with you I cannot attempt any of these things. . . . James Bakewell is not, nor ever will be able to take enough of the care and management of these matters off my hands for me to ingage deeply in them. With him, all I can think of undertaking will be Bronzeing and the black and yellow, and purple enamelling and this not to any extent.'

Some enamelling was done, to Wedgwood's order, by Sadler and Green of Liverpool. Included in this was enamelling with transparent washes of green applied over black transfer prints of sea-shells and flowers (1). Thus we read of '12¾ Doz. small Plates green shell @ 4/6 £2.17.4½' in a bill sent to Wedgwood from Guy Green. Green also enamelled edged borders, etc.

'Liverpool. Sept. 2. 1777.

To Mr. Josiah Wedgwood,
Sir,

By Dan Morris was sent 4½ doz. Dessert Plates Purple edge. My enamellers were about one day in doing a Dozen of them for which they charged me 2/6—I shall be glad to know what you pay as I cannot be persuaded but they must be done a good deal cheaper. I am endeavouring to get the obstacles of their heavy charges removed, by bringing forwards some boys and girls who are now under the care of an Enameller for that purpose.

Yours etc.

Guy Green.'

The edging of Wedgwood's transfer-printed ware in a single enamel colour had been done by Sadler and Green for a long time before the above letter was written, but this letter clearly indicates something more ambitious. For although edging only is mentioned, it would not be likely that Green's enamellers would take a whole day to edge twelve plates. The letter may refer to Wedgwood purple-edged dessert plates with finely-painted flowers in the centre enamelled in a number of other colours (2) and in the same style as some Liverpool enamelling (3). Similar plates but without the flower painting are more commonly found.

Phillips and Greaves, enamellers at Stoke, were responsible for some unidentified painting in blue enamel on Wedgwood's cream-ware about the year 1764.

In 1765, Wedgwood received an order for a creamware tea and

---

(1) *Plate* 85; (2) *Plate* 87B; (3) *Plate* 92B.

coffee service from Queen Charlotte, which is described in a letter written by Josiah to John Wedgwood,

'. . . The order came from Miss Deborah, alias Deb Chetwynd, Sempstress and Laundress to the Queen, to Mr. Smallwood of Newcastle, who brot it to me (I believe because nobody else wod undertake it), & is as follows:—"A complete sett of tea things, with a gold ground and raised flowers upon it in green, in the same manner of the green flowers that are raised upon the *mehons*, so it is wrote, but I suppose it shod be *melons*—The articles are 12 cups for Tea, & 12 saucers, a slop basin, sugar dish wth cover and stand—Teapot & stand, spoon trea—Coffeepot, 12 Coffeecups, 6 pr of hand candlesticks & six melons with leaves, 6 green fruit baskets, and stands edged with gold"—.'

This service, of which not a single specimen is known today, was delivered towards the end of the year 1765, and led to further orders from the Royal family. The Queen's continued patronage prompted Wedgwood to adopt the name 'Queen's Ware' for his creamware. This title for creamware was afterwards adopted by many other potters, but was applied to the pale coloured creamware only.

Mention has been made of Simeon Shaw's statement that Mrs. Warburton of Hot Lane, Cobridge, did some enamelling on early Wedgwood creamware (see page 40), but this has not been verified, and the existing correspondence at Barlaston, between Wedgwood and the Warburtons, only relates to sales of creamware; no mention of enamelling being made.

Of considerable importance was Wedgwood's introduction of creamware decorated with enamelled formal border patterns (1). These prim little designs have an undoubted charm and were painted under the supervision of David Rhodes at Little China Row, Chelsea, from which address on the 4th May, 1770, he was advertising for additional hands to help with the enamelling. This is the type of enamelling most commonly found on Wedgwood's creamware made after 1770.

The identification of enamelling is often difficult, as there was much copying of styles and enamellers frequently moved from one factory or workshop to another if better wages or some other inducement was offered.

Transfer-printing. Creamware decorated with engraved designs transferred from copper plates formed a very large proportion of Wedgwood's creamware. The printing was done by Sadler and Green of Liverpool from September 1761.[1] Some early unsuccessful prints

[1] See E. Stanley Price, *John Sadler a Liverpool Pottery Printer*, West Kirby, 1948.

(1) *Plate* 91B.

are sometimes found on pieces of creamware marked 'Wedgwood', which have been washed over in enamel colours with a very unpleasing effect, but generally the printing was of a high standard from competently engraved plates. The colours used for printing were Indian red (which was not so orange as the Leeds red), jet black and lilac. Among many other engravings which were printed on Wedgwood's creamware, the following subjects may be mentioned:

Portraits	King of Prussia; John Wilkes; John Wesley; Queen Charlotte.
Armorial	The Arms of the Moderns (Masonic) (1); the Arms of the Society of Bucks; the Arms of the Anti-Gallican Society.
Figure Subjects	The Haymakers; Harlequinade (2); Harvest Home; The Tea-party (3); Shepherd (4); various Shepherds and Shepherdesses after Boucher (5); Fables; The Tythe Pig; Hunting scenes (6) and Classical subjects.
Landscapes	Many of these are among the most successful of the prints which occur on Wedgwood's creamware (7).
Birds, Flowers, etc.	

There were many different versions of some subjects, especially of the 'Tea-party'. In one rare version of this, Josiah and Sarah Wedgwood are depicted as the lady and gentleman taking tea. The likenesses are unmistakable (8).

In addition to the subjects already mentioned, some Wedgwood teapots have printed on them on one side 'Aurora' and on the reverse 'The Twelve Houses of Heaven'. These prints, which are washed over in enamel colours, were engraved by William Greatbatch (see pages 30–32), but are unlikely to have been printed by him.

Later Ware. The Etruria factory was established in 1770. The two main classes of creamware made by Wedgwood after this date consisted of vases of classic influence and table-ware painted with formal border patterns. Wedgwood's tortoiseshell and early colour-glazed wares (see page 33) led directly to his manufacture of creamware vases with marbled decoration. It is probable that these were first made in 1768. Vases in uncoloured creamware, and others made of mingled clays in imitation of stones such as onyx, porphyry and granite,

---

(1) *Plate* 75B (cf. *Plate* 60); (2) *Plate* 75A; (3) *Plates* 84, 88B; (4) *Plate* 74; (5) *Plates* 74, 83A; (6) *Plate* 75A; (7) *Plates* 82A, 88A, 89; (8) *Plate* 84.

were made throughout the Wedgwood and Bentley period (1769–80).[1]

The creamware table-ware decorated with enamelled border patterns which were painted at Chelsea (see page 40) (I) was undoubtedly one of Wedgwood's most important contributions to English ceramics, and by reason of its suitability to its purpose has been deservedly popular ever since its first introduction. Not only were the creamware shapes of this ware copied by other potters, but the border patterns were reproduced by a number of English and Continental creamware factories.[2] The Wedgwood ware of this type, which was usually marked, is so well known, and has been referred to at length and illustrated in so many books, that it will not be further discussed here.

The Pattern Books. Wedgwood issued a number of pattern books, which include catalogues of creamware as well as catalogues of ornamental ware. For notes on those relating to creamware, see Appendix II, pages 80, 81.

Figures. Wedgwood himself does not appear to have made any figures in creamware or pearlware, but presumably to meet specific orders he seems to have had a limited number made by the Wood family at Burslem and there impressed with the word 'WEDGWOOD'. The one most commonly found consists of a woman holding a baby and two children. On the front of the base of this figure, the word 'Charity' is impressed and the word 'WEDGWOOD' is impressed at the back. This figure, the modelling of which is typical of the Ralph Woods, is sometimes found decorated with their coloured glazes, but the enamelled creamware version may have been cast and decorated by Enoch Wood. A large enamelled creamware bust of a woman, at the Victoria and Albert Museum, has the word 'Sadness' impressed on the front of its base and the word 'WEDGWOOD' at the back (see Appendix III, Mark 50). This figure is undoubtedly the work of Enoch Wood.

Marks. Prior to 1772 much of Wedgwood's creamware was unmarked, but at this date he wrote to Thomas Bentley proposing that all his ware should be marked. Even after this, however, a great many pieces seem to have been sent out of the factory unstamped. The Wedgwood factory mark on creamware consisted of the word 'Wedgwood' impressed on the ware. This and other Wedgwood marks are discussed and illustrated in Appendix III.

[1] See W. B. Honey, *Wedgwood Ware*, London, 1948, Plates 43 to 47.
[2] Copies of these patterns were made in England by the Spode, Davenport, Ferrybridge and other later creamware factories, which unless marked, are often difficult to distinguish from the Wedgwood originals.

(I) *Plate* 91B.

7

SWINTON AND THE LATER YORKSHIRE FACTORIES

An important group of creamware factories were centred around the principal factory at Leeds. These were for the most part in the South of Yorkshire and were situated on the river Humber and its tributaries the rivers Aire, Calder and Don. Comprehensive collections of the wares from these potteries were left to the Yorkshire Museum at York by Mr. Thomas Boynton and Mr. Arthur Hurst; and valuable contributions to the identification of the wares of these factories, and to our knowledge of the factories themselves, were made by Mr. Oxley Grabham, Mr. Arthur Hurst, Messrs. Joseph and Frank Kidson, and Dr. Maud Sellers.[1]

SWINTON

Two potteries existed at Swinton in the eighteenth century, namely the Swinton Pottery and the Don Pottery.

Swinton lies in the South of Yorkshire, eleven miles north-east of Sheffield. The Swinton Pottery was established in 1745 by Edward Butler. In 1765 William Malpass and John Brameld were partners and subsequently his son William Brameld. In 1778, Thomas Bingley became a partner and the principal proprietor. About 1787 it became associated with the Leeds Pottery and traded under the name 'Greens, Bingley and Co.' and sometime prior to 1796 'Greens, Hartley and Co.'. The Greens were also partners in the Leeds Pottery. This association ended in 1806 and the firm continued under the name 'Brameld and Co.' until 1825, when it was renamed the 'Rockingham Works'.

Jewitt states that the first ware to be made under Edward Butler was a hard brown ware. This was probably similar to the Nottingham brown saltglazed stoneware. He illustrates a two handled posset-cup

---

[1] Oxley Grabham, *Yorkshire Potteries, Pots and Potters*, York, 1916. Arthur Hurst, *Catalogue of the Boynton Collection of Yorkshire Pottery*, York, 1922. Joseph and Frank Kidson, *Historical Notices of the Leeds Old Pottery*, Leeds, 1892. Dr. Maud Sellers, *Yorkshire Pottery* (Victoria County History, Vol. II), 1912.

dated 1759 and authenticated as having been made at the Swinton Pottery. The cup is clearly saltglaze, either brown or white, and has an incised decoration. It would seem that fine white saltglaze was made at Swinton at an early date as well as tortoiseshell ware, and a ware covered with a fine green glaze. Pieces of this last sometimes bear the impressed mark Brameld (see Appendix III, Marks 85 and 86) and are from the same moulds as some white saltglazed stoneware.

Pattern books were issued with the following heading:

'Greens, Hartley & Co., Swinton Pottery, make, sell, and export wholesale all sorts of Earthenware, Cream Coloured or Queen's, Nankeen Blue, Tortoiseshell, Fine Egyptian Black, Brown, China etc. etc. All the above sorts enameled, printed or ornamented with gold or silver.'

On the fly leaf was an announcement of an increase in prices and a revised system of numbering dated 'Swinton Pottery, 1st. February 1796.'

In many instances the designs in the Leeds and Swinton pattern books are similar. Transfer-printing on creamware was done at the Swinton Pottery from some time prior to 1788.

Very little is known of the Swinton creamware of the eighteenth century. Marked pieces are rare and show that the quality was good though less fine than that of the Leeds creamware. The mark 'BRAMELD' in capital letters is occasionally found impressed on creamware.

A teapot (1) transfer-printed in red, with a rose on one side and a flute player on the other, similar to a Liverpool print but in reverse, may be a specimen of Swinton transfer-printing on creamware made at the factory about 1780.

THE DON POTTERY

This pottery which was situated close to the canal at Swinton was founded in 1790 by John Green, manager of the Swinton Pottery and became the largest creamware factory in Yorkshire after the Leeds Pottery. It continued to work until 1893. In 1807 it traded under the name 'Greens, Clarke & Co.'. In 1808 the Don Pottery issued a pattern book, very similar to that issued by the Leeds Pottery but containing more engraved designs. The creamware produced was very inferior to that of the Leeds Pottery and usually showed a lack of finish and considerable crazing. Botanical flower-paintings on creamware dessert services were amongst its best productions. Other types of

---

(1) *Plate* 62A.

ware made by the Don Pottery included transfer-printing on cream-ware, white ware, buff-coloured ware, green-glazed ware and black basalt stoneware. The marks used on the creamware of this factory are illustrated in Appendix III, Marks 87 to 90.

CASTLEFORD POTTERY

Castleford is three miles north of Pontefract at the junction of the rivers Calder and Aire. The pottery was founded about 1790 by David Dunderdale. The creamware was inferior to that of the Leeds pottery. A rather heavy greyish-green glaze is characteristic. A pattern book which shows the great variety of creamware produced by this pottery was issued in 1796 on the lines of that of the Leeds Pottery (see Appendix II, page 82). The ware for which this factory was particu-larly famous was white felspathic stoneware, of which the well known moulded teapots edged with blue enamel were made. The marks used are illustrated in Appendix III, Marks 91 and 92.

ROTHWELL POTTERY

Rothwell is four miles south-east of Leeds. This pottery was founded some time before 1770 when it was being worked by John Smith & Co. Advertisements for the sale of the pot works appear in the *Leeds Mercury* for 13 April 1773 and 3 May 1774. These show that there were three kilns belonging to the pottery; two large warehouses; other 'convenient houses for carrying on the pottery business in the most commodious and extensive manner'; a flint mill; 'a dwelling house for the grinder and 3 spacious rooms, well lighted and fitted up, for the Enamel work', all of which suggests a pottery of some import-ance. It was bought by Samuel Shaw of Staffordshire who worked it for a few years only. The creamware made at this factory is entirely unknown.

PETTY'S POTTERY, HOLBECK MOOR (LEEDS)

This pottery is reputed to have made a fine quality creamware from an early date. In 1792 it was worked by Petty and Rainforth. One or two transfer-printed pieces bearing the mark 'RAINFORTH & CO.' are known (see Appendix III, Mark 93). It is tempting to assign some creamware marked 'HM' (1) to this pottery (see Appendix III, Mark 26).

FERRYBRIDGE POTTERY
(*prior to* 1804, *known as the* KNOTTINGLEY POTTERY)

Pot works were established here in 1792 by William Tomlinson. In 1796, Ralph Wedgwood, a nephew of Josiah Wedgwood, was taken

---

(1) *Plate* 33.

into partnership. Some good quality creamware in imitation of Wedgwood's Queen's ware was made here. The marks used by this factory are illustrated in Appendix III, Marks 94 and 95.

THE STAFFORD POTTERY, STOCKTON-ON-TEES

This pottery, which was established in 1824 or 1825 by William Smith, was situated on the Yorkshire side of the River Tees at Thornaby. It is of interest to collectors of eighteenth-century creamware, chiefly on account of its mark, which sometimes consisted of the word 'WEDGWOOD', or 'WEDGEWOOD' (see Appendix III, Marks 96 to 100). An injunction restraining the Stafford Pottery from using these marks, was granted to the firm of Wedgwood of Etruria in 1848. The wares produced by the Stafford Pottery are stated by Hurst in *A Catalogue of the Boynton Collection of Yorkshire Pottery* to have been 'good ordinary wares for domestic use'.

BELLE VUE POTTERY, HULL

This pottery was founded in 1802 by James and Jeremiah Smith of Hull, Job Ridgway of Shelton, Staffordshire and Josiah Hipwood of Hull. In 1806 the sole proprietors were Job and George Ridgway, and in 1826, the pottery passed into the hands of Mr. William Bell. The pottery was closed in 1841.

The creamware made at the Belle Vue Pottery was very inferior to the best quality creamware. It was clumsily potted and the glaze was usually crazed. Plates with a ship transfer-printed in black upon them are sometimes found with the impressed mark of two bells on the back. Teapots with bell-shaped covers are said to be peculiar to this factory. The factory mark is illustrated in Appendix III, Mark 97.

SWILLINGTON BRIDGE POTTERY

Very little is known about this pottery, which is situated on the River Aire between Leeds and Castleford. Oxley Grabham in *Yorkshire Potteries, Pots and Potters* records that a round creamware plaque with figures in relief and painted in enamel colours, has incised on the back, 'John Wildblood Swillington Bridge Pottery, July 12th, 1831.' It may be that many unidentified plaques of this nature are of Swillington Bridge creamware. A crown impressed is said to be another mark of this factory.

THE LATER STAFFORDSHIRE
POTTERIES

In the same way that the great creamware factory at Leeds had its satellites in Yorkshire, so the Wedgwood factory at Etruria gave the lead to a number of smaller factories in Staffordshire, some of which produced creamware of a very high order. These factories have sometimes been styled plagiarists; but this is doing them an injustice. The creamware produced by them often shows distinctly individual trends and characteristics, and seldom fell to the level of slavish imitation. Towards the end of the eighteenth century the creamware was to a great extent supplanted in Staffordshire by a white ware decorated with transfer-prints in underglaze blue. By about 1820 the manufacture of the blue-printed ware had spread to Yorkshire and elsewhere, and its output at that time far exceeded that of any other class of ware.

NEALE & CO., HANLEY

The creamware made by this pottery seems to have been largely overlooked by collectors and others. In quality of body, glaze and workmanship, if oftens equals the finest productions of the Leeds and Wedgwood factories. It was founded about 1680 by John Palmer, who was one of the pioneers of white saltglazed stone-ware in this country. He was succeeded by his son or grandson Henry Palmer who was probably a saltglaze potter but was better known for his later productions of 'black basalt' and 'jasper-ware' in the style of Wedgwood. John Neale became his partner in 1776. Henry Palmer died in 1778 and Robert Wilson was thereupon engaged by Neale as manager. It seems to have been Wilson who was largely responsible for the beautiful creamware produced by the firm. In 1786 Wilson became a partner.

The creamware produced by Neale & Co. can often be distinguished from that of the Leeds and Wedgwood factories by its peculiar freshness of colour and neatness of execution. This is no doubt partly due to the glaze, which is usually free from all crazing and of a soft pea-green colour of a brighter tint than Wedgwood's glaze. The creamware dessert services made by Neale & Co. are often of the basket work pattern with looped borders painted with 'feathered' edging in cobalt blue, emerald green or sepia enamel colours. Such services usually include a large globular covered bowl on a pedestal foot with pierced sides and surmounted by a knob in the form of a pineapple. Other creamware dessert services are beautifully enamelled with plants copied from herbals with the names of the plants painted on the underside of each piece. Dessert services of this kind were made by the Swansea, Leeds, Wedgwood, Don, Castleford and other factories during the late eighteenth and early nineteenth centuries, but perhaps the finest were made by Neale. These sometimes bear the impressed mark 'NEALE & BAILEY' (Appendix III, Mark 106). Bailey was a partner from 1780. Other types of creamware include fern-pots and stands. These were square-sided, with intertwined snake handles and were either painted with underglaze green or with flowers in enamel colours. There were also sauce-boats formed like a fish, for fish-sauce, and melon-shaped tureens, sometimes painted with blue 'feathered' edging. Much of the Neale creamware was transfer-printed, and was probably done at the factory. Conspicuous is some brilliant rosy purple printing of shells, also some good landscapes and figure subjects in the same colour. Plates with ships transfer-printed in black and coloured over with enamels (1) sometimes bear the impressed mark 'NEALE & CO.' (Appendix III, Marks 102 and 103).[1]

The factory also made an excellent 'pearlware' with a fine blue-tinted glaze of sufficient depth as to give the ware a slightly bluish cast. But it is perhaps best known for its beautiful creamware figures in the neo-classical style of the period, such as the set of 'Seasons' at the Fitzwilliam Museum, Cambridge (2). With their good modelling, neatness of execution and cleanness of appearance, they are among the most charming creamware figures ever made. There are also some excellent figures in pearlware.

In 1802 David Wilson succeeded to the firm which later traded under the name 'D. Wilson & Sons'. For notes and illustrations of the different marks used by this factory, see Appendix III, Marks 102 to 109.

JOHN TURNER OF LANE END

John Turner began by making saltglaze at Stoke. He moved to Lane End in 1762 and became one of the most gifted and capable potters of

---

[1] Somewhat similar plates may be found bearing the impressed marks of such factories as Wedgwood, Herculaneum and Hull.

(1) *Plate* 95A; (2) *Plate* 94A, B.

his time, producing a very great variety of wares which included some excellent creamware and pearlware. Much of Turner's creamware was very similar both in body and glaze to that of the Leeds Pottery and consequently differed from the Wedgwood creamware in the same respects. The usual colour of the glaze was primrose yellow. Unlike the Leeds creamware, however, every edge and corner seems to have been deliberately rounded off, so that it lacks the pleasing sharp and clearcut appearance of Leeds creamware. Much of Turner's creamware was exported to Holland, and Dutch-painted plates bearing the impressed mark 'TURNER' (Appendix III, Mark 121) are not uncommon. Some of these portray the story of the Prodigal Son in enamel painting, while others which were enamelled with a crude but decorative 'Virgin and Child' were sold to pilgrims visiting the shrine at Kevalaar (I). Some of Turner's creamware was enamelled at Yarmouth by Absolon whose name is sometimes found painted on pieces of creamware. Absolon was an independent decorator who obtained creamware in the white for enamelling, not only from Turner, but from Davenport and other factories of the late eighteenth and early nineteenth centuries. His painting was very inferior to the best creamware enamelling and usually consisted of landscapes painted in sepia, sometimes relieved with pale green; or of flowers painted in bright orange monochrome. As well as some unsuccessful enamelling on creamware figures, one of which is at the British Museum, he is also known to have done transfer-printing in black and gilded decoration on glass. Other enamelling on Turner's creamware was usually over-careful and timid although the execution was good.

Some plates marked 'TURNER' were decorated with transfer-prints engraved by John Aynsley of Lane End (see Appendix III, Mark 126 and respective note).[1] Dessert services in pearlware with looped borders and underglaze blue 'feathered' edging are sometimes found with the impressed mark 'TURNER' underneath (see Appendix III, Mark 121). He is also said to have been the first in Staffordshire to print in underglaze blue. Turner died in 1786 and was succeeded by his sons, William and John. The works were closed about 1803.

ELIJAH MAYER OF HANLEY

Elijah Mayer began as an enameller in 1770. A *Directory of*

[1] A well-known engraving by John Aynsley entitled 'Keep within compass' is illustrated in the *Schreiber Collection Catalogue* (Victoria and Albert Museum), Vol. II, Plate 59, No. 411.

(I) *Plate* 96A.

Principal Manufacturers and Merchants in the Counties of Stafford, Chester and Lancaster for 1787 has the following entry:

'Handley—Elijah Mayer, enameller.'

This entry suggests that in 1787 he was an enameller only. Chaffers in *Marks and Monograms* gives the impressed mark 'E. MAYER. 1784'; so that there is no doubt that he was actually potting in 1784. It is probable that he had been making creamware on a small scale for a number of years before 1787, as well as doing his enamelling for which he was better known at that time. This consisted for the main part of copies of Wedgwood's creamware border patterns. The creamware made by Mayer is of good quality, very light in weight, with a clear, apple-green glaze which distinguishes it from most other makes of creamware. Tea-services were frequently fluted, with vertical blue enamelled stripes. Teapots were often straight sided with curved tops and having a simple ball knob on the cover. His name impressed is also sometimes seen on pierced openwork baskets for cakes or fruit, on creamware with an enamelled brown edge and on plates with religious subjects enamelled in Holland. The Hanley and Shelton directory for the year 1818 has the following entry, 'Elijah Mayer & Son, High Street,' showing that at that date Mayer's son Joseph had a share in the business. The works were finally closed in 1830. The marks of Elijah Mayer are illustrated in Appendix III, Marks 117 and 118.

THE WOOD FAMILY OF BURSLEM

This family played a very important part in the history and production of creamware in Staffordshire. There were two main branches of the family which descended from the brothers, Ralph and Aaron Wood sons of Ralph Wood (1677–1753), a miller of Burslem. Ralph Wood (1716–72) and his son Ralph Wood (1748–95) were the makers of the well-known figures decorated with soft underglaze patches of colour. The body and glaze used by the elder Ralph Wood were greyish in colour and perhaps on that account the ware may not be considered to be true creamware except in a broad sense. Unlike the Leeds figures which are glazed throughout, those by the elder Ralph Wood are only glazed on the outside and the hollow interior shows the greyish unglazed body. These were sometimes marked with four trees in relief, being a rebus for Wood (Appendix III, Mark 112). The later figures of this factory which were probably made by the younger Ralph Wood, on the other hand, have a true cream-coloured body; but this also has a greyish appearance, on account of the glaze which is a greyish-blue with a tendency to green. These figures are not open throughout but have a closed base sometimes bearing the impressed mark 'Ra. Wood

Burslem' (Appendix III, Mark 111). Perhaps the best known of the figures made by Ralph Wood the elder and repeated by his son is the 'Vicar and Moses' group. Besides figures and Toby-jugs some marked flower vases occur. In addition to creamware, the Woods also made saltglaze table ware, marked and dated moulds for which are at the Victoria and Albert Museum and British Museum.[1] Brother to the elder Ralph Wood was Aaron Wood (1718–85) the celebrated block-cutter who worked first for Dr. Thomas Wedgwood and from 1746 for Thomas Whieldon. Aaron had two sons, William (1746–1808) and Enoch (1759–1840). William was apprenticed to Josiah Wedgwood in 1762 and continued with the firm of Wedgwood all his life, working first at Burslem and later at Etruria. Much of Josiah Wedgwood's Queen's ware is said to have been moulded by him. Enoch was appren-ticed to Palmer of Hanley and for a time was a partner with his cousin Ralph. In 1783 he commenced as master potter at Fountain Place, Burslem, where he was joined by James Caldwell in 1790, and the firm became 'Wood and Caldwell'. In 1819 he bought Caldwell out, and the firm took the name 'Enoch Wood & Sons', until about 1846, when it was closed. Enoch Wood was a creamware potter and is best known for his figures, which are usually painted in enamel colours. His busts of Wesley, Voltaire and others are familiar and some figures bearing the Wedgwood mark would seem to have been made by him to Wedg-wood's order (see page 42 and Appendix III, Mark 50). In addition to figures, however, Enoch Wood made creamware for the table. Twig-baskets for fruit sometimes bear the mark 'ENOCH WOOD' impressed (Appendix III, Mark 115), and the mark 'W (***)' (Appendix III, Mark 113), which is believed to be his mark is sometimes to be found on pieces from creamware dessert services, such as a large covered pedestal bowl at the Fitzwilliam Museum, Cambridge. The cover of this bowl has the type of flower knob which is illustrated in Appendix I, Plate V, fig. 7.

SHORTHOSE AND HEATH

This factory made a good quality creamware at the end of the eighteenth century though the glaze on much of it shows a consider-able amount of crazing. Cake baskets with pierced openwork sides with the name 'SHORTHOSE' impressed are not uncommon (Ap-pendix III, Marks 127, 128). Dessert-ware was sometimes decorated with transfer-printed designs in red, to which enamelled borders in bright turquoise blue were occasionally added.

[1] A block-mould of a saltglaze cream-jug at the Victoria and Albert Museum is marked 'R.W. 1749'. This mould is illustrated in Bernard Rackham, *Early Staffordshire Pottery*, London, 1951, on Plate 41B.

ENGLISH CREAM-COLOURED EARTHENWARE

WILLIAM ADAMS OF TUNSTALL

A number of potters of the name William Adams, who were descended from William Adams, master potter of Burslem (died 1617), were renowned for printing on creamware in underglaze blue towards the end of the eighteenth century. Of these William Adams of Greengates, Tunstall, who was born in 1745, and worked from 1777–1805, made a fine quality creamware which he painted in underglaze blue. This was very soon superseded however by printing in underglaze blue on pearlware. His name is sometimes found impressed on the ware (Appendix III, Marks 119 and 120). For further information on this family of potters, see, W. Turner, *William Adams an old English Potter*, London, 1904.

JOHN DAVENPORT OF LONGPORT

John Davenport was born in 1765, and worked from 1794 to 1834. He made a good quality whitish creamware frequently painted with landscapes or flowers in a pale bluish-green colour and sepia by Absalon of Yarmouth (see page 49). About 1820 Davenport produced a deep yellow ware and an orange-buff-coloured ware decorated with landscapes painted in black or red. Blue printed ware and a fine quality porcelain were also produced by this factory in the nineteenth century. The factory mark was the name 'DAVENPORT' and an anchor, impressed (see Appendix III, Marks 124 and 125).

JOSIAH SPODE

Josiah Spode was born in 1733. In 1749 he was hired by Thomas Whieldon, and later set up on his own account at Stoke. Spode made a good quality creamware much of which was enamelled with border patterns. These, though often more elaborate, were in much the same style as those found on Wedgwood's creamware.

From 1783 until his death in 1797, Spode's chief manufacture was pearlware printed in underglaze blue and the manufacture of cream-ware seems to have been entirely discontinued. During this period Copeland became a partner with Spode and the firm became 'Spode and Copeland'. After Josiah Spode's death, his son Josiah continued the manufacture of underglaze blue printing, and in 1800 commenced making porcelain. Josiah Spode the second died in 1827 and shortly afterwards the firm traded under the name 'Copeland and Garrett'. The mark used on the creamware of this factory was the name 'SPODE' impressed (Appendix III, Marks 122 and 123).

THE LATER STAFFORDSHIRE POTTERIES

DALE HALL, BURSLEM

This factory was founded by John and George Rogers, about 1780. Besides blue-printed ware, they produced some fine white-ware, decorated with flowers beautifully painted in enamel colours.[1] The name 'ROGERS' is sometimes found impressed on the ware.

LAKIN AND POOLE, BURSLEM

This factory produced some fine quality creamware of a very pale colour towards the end of the eighteenth century. It was sometimes painted with exotic birds in brightly coloured enamels. This pottery also produced an attractive drab-coloured ware enamelled with flowers in black, sepia and white. Figures decorated in enamel colours, blue-printed ware and lustre ware were amongst the other productions of this factory. The usual mark was the name 'Lakin' impressed.

HERBERT MINTON OF STOKE

Among the great variety of wares made by the Minton factory, mention must be made of some undecorated creamware which in form and colour resembled that of the eighteenth century, but which possessed a different composition of body and glaze. This was made by Herbert Minton, about 1840. Such pieces are sometimes impressed with the mark 'H.M. & Co.'

[1] See *Schreiber Collection Catalogue* (Victoria and Albert Museum), Vol. II, Plate 53, No. 429.

9

LIVERPOOL, NEWCASTLE, SUNDERLAND, BRISTOL AND SWANSEA

LIVERPOOL

Very little is at present known of the group of potteries which were situated at Liverpool during the eighteenth century, or their products, but there is little doubt that most of the types of ware produced in Staffordshire were also produced in Liverpool, and that creamware was made there from an early date (1). According to Jewitt the 'Flint Pot Works' were worked by Okell from about 1760 where he made 'blue and white earthenware and afterwards the fashionable cream-coloured ware'. The 'blue and white' probably refers to Delft ware though the possibility of its being scratch-blue saltglaze cannot be altogether disregarded. Okell died in 1773 or 1774 and the works were then taken by Rigg and Peacock who immediately advertised their intention of 'making all kinds of cream-coloured earthenware etc.'. There were undoubtedly other potters making creamware at Liverpool from about 1760, but except for one Statham, who sold cream-ware to John Sadler, and Joseph Johnson,[1] who signed his name on some pieces of his make (Appendix III, Marks 137 and 138), nothing definite seems to be known of them though it has been stated that creamware was made by Chaffers, Barnes, and Seth Pennington. Of importance, however, in the general history of creamware was the firm of Sadler and Green of Liverpool, who decorated a large proportion of Wedgwood's creamware with transfer-printed designs as well as printing delft-ware tiles, saltglaze, porcelain and enamels.

Sadler and Green were printing tiles in 1756 and Wedgwood's

---

[1] This name occurs on a teapot at the Castle Museum, Norwich (Appendix III, Mark 138). The signature of Richard Abbey as the engraver also appears on the same teapot (Appendix III, Mark 136). The name 'I. Johnson, Liverpool' occurs on a small beaker in the Victoria and Albert Museum and is illustrated in the *Schreiber Collection Catalogue*, Vol. II, Plate 61, No. 413.

---

(1) *Plate* 92A.

creamware at the end of the year 1761. Jewitt states that Sadler and Green also made creamware, but this is open to doubt. Although the names Sadler and Green appear on some of the prints, they were not engravers, but printers only. They employed such men as John Evans, Thomas Billinge,[1] and Richard Abbey,[2] who were outside engravers and whose names appear on transfer-printed creamware both of Wedgwood and Liverpool manufacture. It is not always easy to identify the printing of Sadler and Green for they themselves used many variant engravings of the same subject, and very similar prints occur on the creamware of such potteries as Neale and Co., Leeds, and Swinton, the last two of which are known to have done their own printing. Some of the prints from these factories show the subject in reverse, suggesting that they may have been copied from other existing prints. A safer guide than the subject matter can sometimes be found in the quality of printing and the colours used. These, and the subjects printed by Sadler and Green, are referred to in this book in the chapter on Wedgwood. The colours used by other printers is referred to under those factories where transfer-printing was also done. Besides the transfer-printing, Sadler and Green also decorated in enamel colours (see page 39).

HERCULANEUM

In 1793 or 1794 Richard Abbey, the engraver, founded a pottery on the south shore of the Mersey at Toxteth Park for the manufacture of creamware. He took a potter named Graham into partnership, but sold the factory in 1796 to Worthington, Humble and Holland, who named the factory 'Herculaneum'.

The creamware made at the Herculaneum factory is generally inferior in quality to the best creamware, though occasionally pieces with the impressed mark 'HERCULANEUM' (Appendix III, Mark 140) are found which are of a very high standard. Some good early pieces which are almost certainly from this factory have blue enamelled borders and rose pink transfer-printing. Some good enamelling,

---

[1] Thomas Billinge engraved a number of portraits that occur on early Wedgwood creamware teapots as well as the well-known print with the motto 'Let Wisdom Unite Us' (see *Schreiber Catalogue*, Victoria and Albert Museum, Vol. II, Plate 56, No. 404).

[2] A teapot in the Fitzwilliam Museum, Cambridge is decorated with transfer-prints of a dark reddish-brown colour which are signed 'Abbey, Liverpool' (I), (Appendix III, Mark 134). His signature (Appendix III, Mark 136) also occurs on a teapot in the Castle Museum, Norwich, in conjunction with that of Joseph Johnson (see footnote on page 54).

(I) *Plate* 93B.

particularly of landscapes, sometimes occurs on marked pieces, but this type of decoration was soon superseded by blue-printing, black underglaze printing and bat printing. In 1833 the factory traded under the name Case, Mort & Co. and in 1841 it finally closed down.

NEWCASTLE-UPON-TYNE

A group of potteries were founded in Newcastle and its district during the eighteenth and early nineteenth centuries. The first of these is said to have been established between 1730 and 1740 at Carr's Hill Pottery near Gateshead, where white saltglazed stoneware was apparently made.[1] The most important creamware factory in the neighbourhood of Newcastle was at St. Anthony's, and was established about 1780 by Sewell and Donkin. The ware made at this factory was very pale in colour and though in good style is inferior in potting to that of the best creamware. Enamelled flower-painting in the style of Leeds but less vigorous in execution, sometimes occurs on the creamware of this factory, but most of the creamware was left undecorated. The impressed marks used by this factory are illustrated in Appendix III, Marks 141 to 144. Thomas Fell established the St. Peter's Pottery, Newcastle, in 1817. The principal manufacture was white-ware transfer-printed in black under the glaze. Some pearlware plates with green-feathered borders and decorated in mineral colours with birds or landscapes of which the foliage is frequently 'sponged' in, are sometimes found with the impressed mark 'FELL'. This type of decoration was also done at Liverpool and Bristol. The marks of this factory are illustrated in Appendix III, Marks 145 to 147.

SUNDERLAND

About the beginning of the nineteenth century a group of potteries situated on the River Wear near Sunderland were producing a white-ware decorated with transfer-prints and pink lustre. This ware can only be regarded as creamware in the very widest sense. The most important of these factories was the Sunderland Pottery, worked by Dixon, Austin, Phillips & Co. from about 1818. Other potteries in this district were the 'Southwick Pottery' founded in 1789 by Anthony Scott; 'Ford Pottery' (South Hylton) founded in 1800 by John Dawson and the Wear Pottery, which was founded by S. Moore & Co. in 1803. White-ware, transfer-printed in black and washed over in enamel colours with borders of pink lustre, was made by all these factories.

[1] See Llewellyn Jewitt, *The Ceramic Art of Great Britain*, London, 1878.

BRISTOL

Joseph Ring took over the delftware pottery at Temple Back from his father-in-law Richard Frank in 1785, for the manufacture of creamware. Knowing nothing of potting himself he engaged Anthony Hassells of Shelton in 1786 to initiate the manufacture and act as manager. Hassells employed workmen from Staffordshire.[1] The creamware was of a whitish body and though well potted was apt to become stained with use. This staining often gives the ware a some-what dirty appearance, which is further increased by the bluish colour of the glaze. Mugs transfer-printed in umber and coloured over in enamel colours marked 'Bristol Pottery' in the print (Appendix III, Mark 158) were made to celebrate the Treaty of Amiens in 1802 (1). A large obelisk in the Fitzwilliam Museum, Cambridge, bears the same print and mark.

A plate in the Victoria and Albert Museum, having an enamel painted armorial design, is signed 'J. Eaves, Bristol' (Appendix III, Mark 159). Eaves no doubt enamelled for Joseph Ring. It has often been stated that Ring's creamware was of a chalky white body covered with a bright primrose-coloured or yellow glaze. The creamware referred to is of a very high quality, often painted with sprays of flowers in purplish-crimson and sometimes bearing the impressed mark 'HM' (Appendix III, Mark 26) (2). This creamware is almost certainly of Leeds origin and not Bristol. The 'HM' mark has no doubt been confused with the mark 'MH' which occurs on ware made at the Bristol Pottery for the British City Council at a later date. The letters 'MH' stand for 'Mansion House'. After 1788 the firm was 'Ring and Carter' and in 1813 John Pountney became a partner, during which period the little barrels with paintings of flowers by William Fifield were made. M. Powell was another painter of the Pountney period. A modified creamware that had a greyish appearance was made by this factory early in the nineteenth century. It was charmingly decorated in underglaze mineral colours of brown, deep blue, sage-green and orange-buff, and was very similar to some ware made at the Leeds Pottery (see page 23).

SWANSEA

The 'Cambrian Pottery' at Swansea was founded in 1768. About 1790 the pottery was worked by George Haynes and from 1802 till 1813 by L. W. Dillwyn. It is uncertain when creamware was first

---

[1] See W. J. Pountney, *The Old Bristol Potteries*, London and Bristol, 1920.

(1) *Plate* 96B; (2) *Plate* 33.

made at the Cambrian Pottery, but probably not before 1790. Types of creamware made at this factory include dessert services with finely-painted botanical flowers, whose names are inscribed on the back in red enamel, sometimes accompanied by the letter 's', painted in red enamel, or the word 'SWANSEA' impressed. A fine quality pearlware was made by this factory early in the nineteenth century. It was sometimes decorated with beautifully-enamelled butterflies and birds. These were painted by W. W. Young. The glaze on such pieces is usually finely crazed and the ware was greyish in colour. Transfer-printing was done at Swansea. Plates of a thick and heavy creamware which is almost white in colour are sometimes found with the impressed mark 'DILLWYN'. Such plates are often decorated with a ship in jet-black transfer-printing. Other colours used in Swansea transfer-printing are brown and underglaze blue. Many of the plates made by both the Swansea and Bristol factories were edged with black. The Swansea marks are illustrated in Appendix III, Marks 152 to 157.

10

CONTINENTAL CREAMWARE

Creamware was not only the principal manufacture in England between the years 1760 and 1820, completely supplanting the manufacture of white saltglaze by about 1780; but it also played a very important part in the history of European ceramics generally. From about 1760, there was an ever increasing export of English creamware to nearly every European country. Eliza Meteyard in her *Life of Josiah Wedgwood*, London, 1865–6, tells us that between 1770 and 1780 Wedgwood had agents in most European countries. By 1783, the Leeds Pottery was exporting vast quantities of creamware to Germany, Holland, France and Spain as the pattern books published by that factory show. In 1796 the Castleford Pottery published a pattern book written in French and Spanish, and was therefore trading with those countries. Turner of Lane End, the Baddeleys of Shelton and the Warburtons were also exporters on a large scale. In addition potters from Staffordshire, seeing the enormous demand on the Continent for English creamware, left England and set up factories in France itself. All this activity threatened the very life of the Continental faïence factories and undercut the sale of porcelain as well. In self-defence, they turned from their long established traditions, to the manufacture of creamware; and by the end of the eighteenth century, creamware was being made by every country in Europe. In France creamware was known as 'Grès d'Angleterre', 'Faïence fine', or 'Faïence anglaise'; in Germany it was 'Steingut' and in Sweden 'Flintporslin'. Although a number of Continental factories advertised the fact that they deliberately copied the English creamware, in point of fact the Continental and English creamwares often bore little resemblance to each other . Many Continental factories followed their own traditions and developed types of ware in an idiom entirely their own, in order to satisfy their own particular needs or requirements. For example, the use of large tureens, to hold a mixed dish or hot-pot, was much more general in some Continental countries, than in England, consequently countries such as France or Sweden produced large quantities of handsome creamware tureens, which were pieces of importance, often superbly modelled in the rococo manner, and were altogether more ambitious than the English counterparts, though the technique and finish were inferior to that of the best creamware made in this country.

The collector of English creamware may be sometimes puzzled by certain pieces in his collection which are conspicuous by reason of their somewhat different appearance. Such pieces frequently prove to be of Continental origin. The subject of 'Continental Creamware' has been very little studied either on the Continent or in England, but a few brief notes on the more important European creamware factories and their wares are subjoined, in the hope that they will be helpful in such cases.

Perhaps the earliest and most important French factory to manufacture a kind of creamware was the *Pont-aux-Choux* factory at Paris. This was founded in 1743 by Claude Humbert Gérin, who was succeeded in 1747 by Mignon, for the manufacture of 'faïence fine' in imitation of English ware. In 1743 creamware in England was only in its infancy but saltglaze was firmly established and there is no doubt that saltglaze was the English ware that was first copied in France. This is borne out by specimens of Pont-aux-Choux manufacture which in colour and general appearance closely resemble English saltglaze,[1] but which, upon closer inspection, would appear to have been glazed with lead. In fact, they have characteristics of both saltglaze and creamware. The creamware made by this factory never seems to have been enamelled, but was decorated with well-moulded floral designs in low relief, which were derived from English saltglaze models. Another type of decoration used extensively by the Pont-aux-Choux factory was the 'barleycorn' pattern, which was a much used pattern on English saltglaze.[2] Amongst the productions of the Pont-aux-Choux factory may be mentioned the large tureens, in the rococo style, the shapes of which were based on silver prototypes. These were magnificent pieces with elaborate covers which were sometimes surmounted by modelled birds, fruit and flowers. (Illustrated in *English Ceramic Circle Transactions*, Vol. 3, Part 4, Plate 71C.) In addition the Pont-aux-Choux factory produced jardinieres; jugs; covered mugs and bowls; vases for pot-pourri; sauce-boats with or without covers, and figures some of which depicted Chinese men and women bearing sconces to hold candles. In 1772 the Pont-aux-Choux factory advertised itself as 'Manufacture royale des terres de France à l'imitation de celles d'Angleterre'. These wares, however, are readily distinguishable from the English. The date of the closure of the Pont-aux-Choux fac-

---

[1] Although the ware made at the Pont-aux-Choux factory was generally the whitish colour of English saltglaze, occasionally pieces are found which have a decided tinge of pink.

[2] Saltglaze block-moulds of table-ware decorated with the 'barleycorn' pattern are at the Wedgwood Museum, Barlaston, and were used in the manufacture of Wedgwood saltglazed stoneware.

tory is not known, but Mignon was still head of the factory in 1786 and it was still working in 1798.

In 1780 two English potters named Charles and Jacob Leigh, who were Roman Catholics, fled to France in order to avoid the violence of the Puritans. In 1781, they founded a factory at *Douai* for the production of 'fayence en grès pâte tendre blanche connue sous le nom de grès d'Angleterre'. The ware was not so thick as that produced by the Pont-aux-Choux factory. At first it was ivory-coloured and of good quality, and was sometimes decorated with pierced open-work designs. Later a white-ware was made which was sometimes painted with flowers, religious scenes, masonic emblems or inscriptions in monochrome or polychrome enamel colours. The factory closed in 1831. The ware was mostly unmarked but pieces are sometimes found with 'LEIGH' or 'DOUAI' impressed. Another factory at Douai, which made similar types of ware, was founded in 1799 by Martin Damman. This factory only lasted for eight years.

In 1786 faïence fine was being made at *Chantilly*. The ware had a slightly matt appearance and was the colour of English white saltglaze, which it resembled more closely than English creamware. Gilding, especially in lines and in small spotted motifs, seems to have been a favourite form of decoration. Chantilly teapots sometimes have a knob formed of three flowers, as on some porcelain examples from the same factory. The factory mark was a hunting-horn or a fleur-de-lis in colour. In 1792 the factory was sold to Christopher Potter, an Englishman, who manufactured white-ware, the shapes of which were derived from Wedgwood's creamware. This ware was sometimes enamelled in blue or was transfer-printed. Creamware ceased to be made at Chantilly in 1820.

The factory at *Lunéville* produced some large well-modelled figures. A bust of Louis XV in a rich butter-coloured creamware is at the Victoria and Albert Museum.

In 1748 Mazois was manufacturing earthenware in imitation of English saltglaze at *Montereau*. At this date his partner Jean Hill, an Englishman, came to England to discover the process of English saltglaze manufacture. The next year Mazois was making red, black and agate wares, which processes he had learnt in England. In 1756, he had an English partner by the name of Warburton. At this time he was still experimenting with saltglaze. Mazois died in 1774 and the factory was let to an English company directed by William Clark and George or Ralph Shaw.[1] A few years later this firm opened another

[1] The name George Shaw is given by the French authorities, Messelet and Haumont. George may have been the son of Ralph Shaw and possibly succeeded his father as director (or manager) of the firm. Solon, *French Faïence*, gives Ralph

factory at *Creil*. The ware produced by the Montereau and Creil factories from this time was a whiteware which was transfer-printed in black in Paris by Stone, Cocquerel and Le Gros, who added their printed mark. The usual subjects for the engravings of these prints were French or English country houses, and classical, biblical or historic scenes. The ware is often marked 'CREIL' or 'MONTEREAU' impressed.

After the dissolution of the partnership between Peter and Francis Warburton, Peter became a partner of the New Hall works in Staffordshire, while in 1802 Francis set up a factory at *La Charité-sur-Loire* (Nièvre), for the manufacture of white-ware, some of which was marked 'LA CHARITÉ' impressed. Landscapes painted in black and dark brown are found on the creamware of the *Bellevue* factory near Toul, and a yellowish creamware was made at *Apt*. In general the French creamware was heavier and less refined than the English. The glazes also differed from those used in this country both in quality and colour.

The chief creamware factory in Belgium was at *Andenne*, where a factory was founded in 1783 by Joseph Wouters. The ware produced was white decorated with enamel painting or transfer-printing in blue. The factory mark was 'ADW' impressed.

In Germany the factory at *Durlach* produced creamware some of which was decorated with vine leaf borders either painted in black or brown, or moulded in relief. The factory mark was 'DURLACH' impressed. The creamware made at *Hubertusberg* at the end of the eighteenth century was sometimes marked 'WEDGWOOD' impressed. At *Königsberg* (East Prussia), John Ehrenreich made creamware from 1772. A border pattern of shells picked out in blue is typical of the form of decoration used by this factory. The mark was the letter 'K' impressed.

Between 1786 and 1827 the *Holitsch* factory in Hungary made a medium-quality creamware which was either decorated with pierced openwork borders or enamelled with conventional patterns. The mark was the name 'HOLITSCH' or the letter 'H' impressed. Some black transfer-printing on a coarse white-ware was done at *Luxembourg*. Creamware was made at *Marieberg* in Sweden, towards the end of the eighteenth century. The influence of English saltglaze showed itself

---

Shaw of Burslem, manager with W. Clark of Newcastle-under-Lyme. Ralph Shaw of Burslem left for Paris in 1736 as a result of his losing a law case which he brought against another potter for the infringement of a patent (see Josiah C. Wedgwood, *Staffordshire Pottery and its History*, London, 1914, p. 58). Ralph Shaw whilst at Burslem made slipware and sgraffito ware on which patterns were made by cutting away the slip to reveal the contrasting colour of the body underneath. Simeon Shaw in his *History of the Staffordshire Potteries*, Hanley, 1829, states that Ralph Shaw glazed his ware with salt. If this was the case, a form of saltgaze may have been introduced into France soon after 1736.

on some large creamware tureens with flowers moulded in low relief. It is said that stamped ornaments from metal moulds similar to those used in England, were also used by this factory. The ware itself was much lighter in weight than that made by most Continental factories. The Marieberg factory also produced some transfer-printed ware. The factory mark was '$\frac{STEN}{MB}$' impressed. In Denmark the *Gudumland* factory was worked between 1804 and 1814 by Count Schimmelmann. Three brown spots were used as a mark on the creamware of this factory between 1808 and 1814. The factory was closed in 1820.

Very little is known of the creamware that was made in Italy, but several examples which were made at *Naples* are exhibited at the Victoria and Albert Museum as well as a fine coffee-pot from *Le Nove*. The two main factories at Naples were conducted by the Vecchio family and the Giustiniani family. The ware made at the former factory is nearly white in colour and is of fine quality. The decorations for the most part consist of elaborate enamel painting, which is more pictorial than decorative. The factory mark is 'F.D.V.N.' standing for F. del Vecchio, Napoli. The ware made by the Guistiniani family at Naples about 1815 is of a rich cream colour, decorated with pierced openwork. This ware is thicker than the Leeds creamware, though nearly resembling it in other respects. Such ware is sometimes marked 'BG' impressed, standing for Biagio Giustiniani. The Le Nove coffee-pot closely approaches the quality of the finest English creamware though differing in shape, detail and decoration. The Victoria and Albert Museum specimen has plain double intertwined handles without terminals. The pot is skilfully enamelled with a scene inspired by the paintings of Watteau, which though perhaps slightly over-pictorial is nevertheless very good decoration. This coffee-pot is marked with the letters '$\frac{G.M}{B}$' impressed which stand for Giovanni Maria Baccin. A star in red enamel also occurs as a mark of this factory. Mention must be made of an interesting potter and decorator of *Savona*, named Giacomo Boselli, alias Jacques Boselly. His enamelling is usually in brick red or brown. Specimens of creamware made by the Leeds and Wedgwood factories were also enamelled and signed by him. His signature, which is usually painted in brown, consists of the name 'Giacomo Boselli' or the French form 'Jacques Boselly'. A plate at the Victoria and Albert Museum which is transfer-printed in red, is signed 'Jacques Bosselly'.

In Spain during the early nineteenth century, creamware was manufactured at *Alcora*. Some beautifully modelled figure groups, of a rich cream-colour, were amongst the productions of this factory.

Appendix I

HANDLES, SPOUTS AND KNOBS

Much help in identifying the origin of creamware may be gained by a comparison of some of the moulded details. From a close study of the pattern-books and of marked specimens it has been discovered that there exists a remarkable consistency in the details of designs used by particular factories. Even when different factories used closely similar designs, these are seldom identical.

PLATE I. SPOUTS

Plate I, fig. 1. The *Crabstock* or *Crabtree* spout (1) accompanied by a similar handle (Plate III, fig. 1), was first introduced on saltglaze teapots and punch-pots about 1745, though it had earlier prototypes. It is found also on unglazed red-ware, glazed black-ware and colour-glazed ware of the 'Whieldon' type, and was naturally adopted as the earliest form of spout on creamware made in Staffordshire, at Leeds, Liverpool and Derby. Although the handle on the cover of saltglaze teapots was often of crabstock form, except for a very few early examples, this was replaced on creamware teapots by a ball, mushroom, or flower-shaped knob. Crabstock spouts and handles ceased to be made about 1770.

Plate I, fig. 2. Hexagonal or Facetted spout, with small moulded ornamentations, c. 1763–77 (2). This spout was normally accompanied by the Facetted loop handle (Plate III, fig. 5) but it frequently occurs with other types of handle, particularly the 'Scroll' handle (Plate III, fig. 3B). It was probably first modelled by W. Greatbatch for Whieldon and Wedgwood (3) (see page 26), but was much more extensively made at Cockpit Hill, Derby.

Plate I, fig. 3. Plain Hexagonal or Facetted spout, c. 1763–77 (4). Although this spout was used extensively on saltglaze, as far as is known the only creamware examples of it are of Cockpit Hill, Derby, origin.

Plate I, fig. 4. Rococo spout, c. 1760–85 (5). There were several slight variations of this spout but they would all appear to be of Leeds

---

(1) *Plate* 8A; (2) *Plates* 8B, 10A, B; (3) *Plate* 71A; (4) *Plate* 9A; (5) *Plate* 14B.

origin, though the possibility of some having been made at Liverpool must not be overlooked. A marked example is at the Leeds City Art Gallery. This is illustrated in Donald C. Towner, *Handbook of Leeds Pottery*, 1951, No. 76.

Plate I, fig. 5. Fern pattern, *c.* 1760–70 (1). Known examples of this spout would all appear to be of Leeds origin. It was often used in conjunction with the handle, Plate IV, fig. 4.

Plate I, fig. 6. Floral pattern, *c.* 1765–75 (2). This pattern was probably only used at Cockpit Hill, Derby, and was usually accompanied by the handle, Plate III, fig. 3B.

Plate I, fig. 7. Fluted spout with leaves at the base, *c.* 1760–80 (3). This type of spout seems to have been in general manufacture. Examples from Staffordshire and Leeds are known.

Plate I, fig. 8. Twisted spout, *c.* 1760–70. This was one of the earliest types of Leeds spout. It was often used in conjunction with the twisted handle, Plate IV, fig. 5.

Plate I, fig. 9. Straight spout, *c.* 1770 (4). This type of creamware spout was made at the Leeds Pottery where it was sometimes accompanied by the handle, Plate IV, fig. 7. It was also made in unglazed red-ware and black basalt ware by other factories.

PLATE II. SPOUTS (*continued*)

Plate II, fig. 1. Cabbage or Cauliflower spout, *c.* 1760–80 (5). This spout, which was used very extensively by Wedgwood, was probably modelled in the first place by William Greatbatch for Wedgwood's cauliflower ware (see page 27). Examples of this spout also occur in saltglaze. It was copied by a number of other factories. Wedgwood examples on creamware are always accompanied by one of the following handles, Plate III, fig. 3. Plate III, fig. 3A. Plate IV, fig. 1. Plate IV, fig. 2. Plate IV, fig. 3.

The type of Wedgwood spout which occurs on Wedgwood's earliest transfer-printed ware, though not illustrated in the Appendix, is shown on the British Museum teapot (6). The original mould for this spout is in the Wedgwood Museum, Barlaston.

Plate II, fig. 2. Shell, *c.* 1764–85. This spout was modelled in 1764 by William Greatbatch for Wedgwood (see page 28) who used it for both teapots and coffee-pots (7). It was used by Wedgwood in conjunction with the handle, Plate IV, fig. 3. It was later copied by the Leeds Pottery, as some teapots, *c.* 1785, which have this spout are marked 'LEEDS * POTTERY'.

---

(1) *Plate* 15A; (2) *Plate* 9B; (3) *Plates* 28, 81; (4) *Plates* 15B, 22A; (5) *Plate* 75A; (6) *Plate* 75B; (7) *Plate* 85.

Plate II, fig. 3. Simple Shell spout, *c.* 1764–85 (1). This spout may have been modelled by William Greatbatch for Wedgwood or Whieldon. A spout of this pattern was excavated at Fenton Low, and is now at the Castle Museum, Norwich. It was first used by Wedgwood for creamware covered with a green glaze, an example of which is at the Fitzwilliam Museum, Cambridge. It was accompanied by the handle (Plate III, fig. 4), both for green-glazed ware and creamware. It was copied by the Leeds Pottery as some teapots, *c.* 1785, which have this spout are marked 'LEEDS ∗ POTTERY'.

Plate II, fig. 4. Spout with enfolding acanthus at base, *c.* 1775–80. This spout occurs on Leeds pottery and is usually accompanied by the handle, Plate IV, fig. 8, and knob, Plate V, fig. 4. It is not known to have been used by any other factory.

Plate II, fig. *5.* Spout with acanthus at base, *c.* 1770–1815 (2). This spout was very extensively used by the Leeds Pottery. It is shown in the pattern books and specimens marked 'LEEDS ∗ POTTERY' are known. With the possible exception of Swinton, it does not appear to have been used on any other eighteenth-century creamware, but it may have been copied by other factories in the early nineteenth century. It is usually accompanied by the handle, Plate IV, fig. 8, and knob, Plate V, fig. 4.

Plate II, fig. 6. Fluted spout springing from a fluted base, *c.* 1775–1785 (3). This type of spout appears to have been made at the Leeds Pottery only.

Plate II, figs, 7, 8, 9, c. 1775–85 (4). These three spouts were used in conjunction with the indented curve or ear-shaped handle, Plate III, fig. 6, and either the flower knob, Plate V, fig. 1, or a pierced ball knob. Teapots with these characteristics are often decorated with black transfer-prints coloured over with enamel, some of which are signed by William Greatbatch (see page 30). The spouts, Plate II, figs. 7, 8, however, were sometimes used not only in conjunction with the above handle and flower knob, but also in conjunction with the handle, Plate IV, fig. 8, and flower knob, Plate V, fig. 4, on teapots decorated in enamel colours only. These must be considered to be of Leeds origin (see notes under Plates IV, fig. 8 and V, fig. 4). The spout, Plate II, fig. 9, only seems to occur on the coloured transfer-printed teapots, and though probably of Leeds origin, its attribution is less certain.

In addition to the spouts shown on Plate I and II, two creamware moulds for spouts, which were taken from the Leeds Pottery by Kidson, are illustrated (5).

---

(1) *Plate 77*A; (2) *Plate 31*A; (3) *Plate 34*B; (4) *Plates 64*A, 65A, 66B; (5) *Plate 44.*

PLATE III. HANDLES

Plate III, fig. 1. Crabstock or Crab-tree, *c.* 1745–70 (1). This handle was usually accompanied by the 'Crabstock' spout and was of general manufacture (see notes on the Crabstock spout, Plate I, fig. 1).

Plate III, fig. 2. Flat-loop or Strap handle, *c.* 1745–70 (2). This handle was used for coffee-pots, chocolate-pots, jugs and mugs, but never seems to have been used for teapots. It is the earliest form of handle to be found on creamware of these descriptions. It originated in saltglaze about 1740 and was also used for unglazed red-ware, glazed black-ware and solid agate ware. Although it is often associated with the work of Thomas Whieldon, it was used by other potters as well, and there are known examples of Leeds, Liverpool, and Derby origin besides those of Staffordshire. Plate III, fig. 2*a* is a variation of the pinched end.

Plate III, fig. 3. Scroll handle, *c.* 1760–70. There were a number of variations of the 'Scroll' handle, of which four of the most usual types are illustrated (Plate III, figs. 3, 3*a*, 3*b*, 3*c*). The earliest of these, Plate III, fig. 3, was used by Wedgwood for his first transfer-printed creamware of 1761 (3). It was, however, quickly copied by other factories and used to a limited extent at Leeds and possibly Liverpool. The Wedgwood examples are usually sharper in modelling than the copies. It is also to be found on ware with mottled glazes of Wedgwood origin. It was used for teapots and coffee-pots and was usually accompanied by the cauliflower spout and pierced ball or mushroom knob on Wedgwood creamware. On Leeds creamware, it was sometimes accompanied by the spout, Plate I, fig. 7.

Plate III, fig. 3a. Scroll handle, *c.* 1765–75 (4). This variation of the 'Scroll' handle was first used by Wedgwood for creamware a few years later than the previous one, and is to be found on early Wedgwood teapots made before *c.* 1775, where it is usually accompanied by the 'cauliflower' spout (Plate II, fig. 1) and pierced ball knob. It was also used by Wedgwood for his cauliflower teapots. Though this variety of the scroll handle may have been used by other Staffordshire potters who were closely associated with Wedgwood, it is essentially a Wedgwood handle.

Plate III, fig. 3b. Scroll handle, *c.* 1765–75. This variety of the scroll handle was adopted by the Leeds and Derby factories in close imitation of the Wedgwood variety (Plate III, 3*a*). Although it is not usually found on Leeds creamware, it figures in the Leeds drawing books (Plate IX). It was used a great deal by the Cockpit Hill, Derby,

---

(1) *Plate* 14A; (2) *Plate* 20; (3) *Plate* 75B; (4) *Plate* 76B.

factory, usually accompanied by spouts, Plate I, figs. 2, 3, or 6, and a small pierced knob like a button (1).

Plate III, fig. 3c. Scroll handle, *c.* 1765–75. This variety of the scroll handle occurs on the creamware of the Cockpit Hill, Derby factory where it was used in conjunction with the spout, Plate I, fig. 2, and on some teapots with mottled glazes. Some teapots with this handle may be of Staffordshire origin.

Plate III, fig. 4. Simple loop. From *c.* 1760 (2). This handle was first introduced by Wedgwood for his green-glazed creamware on which it was accompanied by the 'Shell' spout (see note for Plate II, fig. 3). Although variations of it have been made by most factories ever since, it seems to have been discarded by Wedgwood, in this particular form, about 1770.

Plate III, fig. 5. Facetted loop, *c.* 1763–77 (3). This handle which was usually accompanied by the facetted spout (Plate I, figs. 2 and 3) was probably first modelled by William Greatbatch for Whieldon and Wedgwood (see page 26). It was extensively used at Cockpit Hill, Derby, where in some instances the small moulded patterns on it were omitted (4). Examples also occur on ware decorated with coloured glazes.

Plate III, fig. 6. Indented loop, *c.* 1770–85. This handle was probably first made by Wedgwood. A mug (5) of Wedgwood's creamware, dating from about 1770, has a handle of this type. It also appears on some Wedgwood creamware of a slightly later date, but it was used to a much greater extent by the Leeds Pottery, and it was almost certainly made at Liverpool as well. On Leeds creamware it is usually accompanied by the spout, Plate II, fig. 7, and occasionally by the spouts, Plate II, figs. 4, 5, or 6. Nearly all the teapots with coloured transfer-printed decoration engraved by William Greatbatch have this type of handle except those made by Wedgwood. The former are almost certainly of Leeds origin (see under Plate II, figs. 7, 8, 9).

PLATE IV. HANDLES (*continued*)

Plate IV, fig. 1. Loop with overlapping scales, *c.* 1770–90 (6). This was the handle most generally adopted by Wedgwood for teapots and jugs. It does not appear to have been made by any other factory. It was used in conjunction with the 'cauliflower' spout (Plate II, fig. 1).

Plate IV, fig. 2. Plain loop with curled base, *c.* 1770–90 (7). This handle denotes a Wedgwood origin, but is much more rare than the double variety (see Plate IV, fig. 3). It was used for teapots and jugs.

(1) *Plate* 9B; (2) *Plate* 77A; (3) *Plate* 71B; (4) *Plate* 9A; (5) *Colour Plate* D; (6) *Plate* 84; (7) *Plate* 76B.

On teapots it was accompanied by the 'cauliflower' spout (Plate II, fig. 1) and pierced ball knob.

Plate IV, fig. 3. Double intertwined handle with curled extremities, *c.* 1775–90. This handle was used by Wedgwood for teapots, coffee-pots and jugs. He also used a very similar handle for cups. It may have been copied and made to a limited extent by Leeds and Enoch Wood. Though usually accompanied by the 'cauliflower' spout (Plate II, fig. 1), it is sometimes found in conjunction with the 'shell' spout (Plate II, fig. 2) (1).

Plate IV, fig. 4. Double intertwined handle, joined at the base, *c.* 1770 (2). This handle was made at the Leeds Pottery for teapots and was usually accompanied by the 'fern' spout (Plate I, fig. 5). It does not appear to have been used by any other factory.

Plate IV, fig. 5. Double intertwined and twisted handle, the ends covered by terminals, *c.* 1770 (3). This was a type of handle made at the Leeds Pottery for coffee-pots and teapots.

Plate IV, fig. 6. Reeded loop with foliate base, *c.* 1770 (4). This is a Wedgwood pattern, the mould for which, dated 1768, is in the Wedgwood Museum, Barlaston. It is not known to have been made by any other factory. It is sometimes accompanied by the spout, Plate I, fig. 7.

Plate IV, fig. 7. Double intertwined handle with foliate ends, *c.* 1770 (5). This occurs on teapots of Leeds manufacture, but is rare. It is sometimes associated with a straight spout (Plate I, fig. 9).

Plate IV, fig. 8. Reeded double intertwined handle with terminals, *c.* 1775–1815 (6). This handle was used very extensively at Leeds for teapots, coffee-pots, jugs, mugs, etc. It is shown in the Leeds drawing books and pattern books (Plate VIII, fig. 12). The usual terminals used for this handle are Plate VI, figs. 4, 5, 11, 13. It is usually accompanied by spouts, Plate II, figs. 4, 5, 6, and flower knobs, Plate V, figs. 4, 4*a*, 4*b*, 4*c*. This handle when used in conjunction with the terminals enumerated above, does not appear to have been made by any other factory with the possible exception of Swinton. It should be noted that the Leeds handles are more finely reeded than those of other factories, the number of reeds being seldom less than five and sometimes as many as eleven.

Plate IV, fig. 9. Double intertwined handle with foliate ends, *c.* 1780–1820 (7). This handle and another which has foliate ends of a slightly different pattern seem to be peculiar to the Leeds Pottery and were used extensively on the later creamware. They are both illus-

---

(1) *Plates* 85, 87A; (2) *Plate* 15A; (3) *Plates* 14B, 22A; (4) *Plate* 81 (5) *Plate* 15B; (6) *Plate* 36; (7) *Plate* 61.

trated in the Leeds pattern book (Plate VII, fig. 65, etc. and Plate VIII, fig. 6). They were used for coffee-pots, teapots, jugs, mugs, cups, etc.

PLATE V. FLOWER KNOBS

Plate V, figs. 1, 1a, 1b. Convolvulus with frilled edge, *c.* 1765–85. The same flower knob is shown in each of these three drawings, but the terminals differ. A drawing of a covered jug in one of the Leeds drawing books, shown on Plate IX, is probably intended to represent fig. 1*a.* This knob may have been used at Swinton as well (1). Fig. 1*b,* occurs on Leeds creamware made before 1775. Fig. 1, occurs on Leeds enamelled creamware (2) as well as on teapots with engravings by William Greatbatch (3). It is usually accompanied by the handle, Plate III, fig. 6, and the spouts, Plate II, figs. 7, 8, 9 (see under Plate II, figs. 7, 8, 9 for additional notes).

Plate V, figs. 2, 2a. Convolvulus, *c.* 1770 (4). Fig. 2*a* shows the same flower as fig. 2, but in fig. 2*a* the edge has been cut to form petals (5). This knob was used by the Leeds Pottery before 1775. Some very similar knobs were made by the Pont-aux-Choux factory at Paris (see page 60).

Plate V, figs. 3, 3a. Convolvulus with straight markings, *c.* 1765–1775 (6). This flower knob seems to have been made at the Leeds Pottery only. Sometimes the accompanying applied terminal is of a different pattern.

Plate V, figs. 4, 4a, 4b, 4c. Flower with terminal of two buds, *c.* 1770–1820 (7). This is the usual flower knob found on Leeds teapots made after 1775, though it occasionally occurs on the earlier deep cream Leeds teapots as well (8). It is the type of flower knob usually depicted in the Leeds pattern-books (Plates VII, VIII). It is usually accompanied by the handle, Plate IV, fig. 8, and one of the spouts, Plate II, figs. 4, 5, 6 (see under these for additional notes). The flower is made in two parts, a flat button-like form being superimposed upon a conical form with a nick at the base. This construction seems to be peculiar to the Leeds Pottery. The flower, fig. 4*c,* was used to decorate the figure-group in the Victoria and Albert Museum (9). Fig. 4*a* is believed to have been used at Liverpool, but with a different terminal. Some nineteenth-century copies of this knob occur on pots marked 'Wedgwood'. These lack the sharpness of the Leeds originals.

Plate V, fig. 5. Reflex flower with spiral centre, *c.* 1775–85. This flower occurs on coffee-pots of Leeds manufacture both in plain or

---

(1) *Plate* 62A; (2) *Plate* 35A and B; (3) *Plate* 66B; (4) *Colour Plate* A; (5) *Plate* 26B; (6) *Plates* 14B, 24; (7) *Plates* 34A, 36; (8) *Plate* 15A; (9) *Plate* 54.

enamelled creamware (1) and in tortoiseshell ware (2). It was also used by the Wedgwood factory though with a different terminal for some tea ware made during the early nineteenth century and for covered openwork cake-baskets during the nineteenth and twentieth centuries. The usual eighteenth-century Wedgwood knob for these is shown on Plate V, fig. 8.

Plate V, fig. 6. Convolvulus, *c.* 1770–85 (3). This is another type of flower knob which, except for some made by the Pont-aux-Choux factory at Paris, seems to be peculiar to the Leeds Pottery.

Plate V, fig. 7. The spiral centre, *c.* 1780–1820 (4). This flower knob differs from the preceding knobs with spiral centres in that each one was made separately; the petals were attached separately and a spiral coil applied to the centre. It was mostly used for covered bowls. Though some pieces with this flower knob appear to have been made by the Leeds Pottery, a large covered bowl with this knob, in the Fitzwilliam Museum, Cambridge, is impressed 'W(***)', which mark is usually associated with Enoch Wood. A similar flower knob is believed to have been occasionally used by Wedgwood.

Plate V, fig. 8. Wedgwood flower knob. *c.* 1770–1820 (5). This flower knob was used very extensively by Wedgwood for teapots, coffee-pots, covered jugs, covered bowls, dishes, etc. It does not appear to have been made by any other factory. On teapots it was usually accompanied by the spouts, Plate II, figs. 1 or 2, and the handle, Plate IV, fig. 3.

Plate V, fig. 9. Rose, *c.* 1775–1800 (6). This is a Wedgwood knob. It does not seem to have been used to the same extent as Plate V, fig. 8, nor does it appear to have been made by any other factory. It seems to have been used for smaller pots than the previous one such as small covered jugs and butter-dishes.

Plate V, fig. 10. Convolvulus, without applied terminal, *c.* 1770 (7). This flower knob is of Leeds origin and is sometimes accompanied by the handle, Plate IV, fig. 7, and the straight spout, Plate I, fig. 9.

PLATE VI. TERMINALS

A great number of different terminals were used on creamware to cover the join of handles and knobs to the pot. Those illustrated on Plate VI, though only a small selection, are those of most usual occurrence. Most of the applied terminals were made at the Leeds Pottery.

Plate VI, figs. 1, 2, 3, 6, 7, 8. This type of terminal in which a form of berry between leaves is conspicuous, is found on the deep cream-coloured ware of the Leeds Pottery made before 1775 (8). It was used

---

(1) *Plate* 37; (2) *Plate* 38; (3) *Plates* 28, 31B; (4) *Plate* 63A; (5) *Plates* 85, 88B, 91A; (6) *Plate* 90B; (7) *Plate* 15B; (8) *Plates* 19B, 29.

on teapots, coffee-pots, jugs, tureens, etc. Plate VI, fig. 3, however, is from a fragment taken from the site of the Fenton Low Pot-works (collection of Mr. A. T. Morley Hewitt), and is the terminal to a double intertwined handle. Though very similar in type, it is not identical in design with known Leeds patterns. The flower with only five petals is an unusual feature. The other terminals shown in this group are all from pieces of Leeds creamware.

Plate VI, fig. 4, occurs on Leeds creamware but may have been used at Swinton as well (1).

Plate VI, fig. 5, occurs on Leeds creamware of both the deep and pale colours. It is not known on the ware of any other factory.

Plate VI, figs. 9, 10, 14, 15. These small terminals occur on small pieces of Leeds creamware and are illustrated in the Leeds pattern and drawing books. Fig. 15, occurs on Plate IX of Appendix II.

Plate VI, fig. 11. This terminal was used very extensively by the Leeds Pottery from *c.* 1775–1820. It is frequently shown in the pattern book (Appendix II, Plate VIII, fig. 12), and occurs on marked pieces. It is not known on the ware of any other factory (2).

Plate VI, fig. 12. This terminal was used by the Leeds Pottery in conjunction with the flower knob, Plate V, fig. 6, and spout, Plate I, fig. 7, *c.* 1780 (3). It is not known on the ware of any other factory.

Plate VI, fig. 13. This terminal occurs on Leeds creamware *c.* 1765–90 (4). It is not known on the ware of any other factory.

Plate VI, fig. 16. This terminal occurs on undoubted Leeds creamware (5) of *c.* 1780 as well as on the covers of teapots bearing prints engraved by William Greatbatch and coloured over in enamels. These are also probably of Leeds origin, but the attribution is less certain (see page 30 and under Plate II, figs. 7, 8, 9). Fig. 16 was mostly used in conjunction with the flower knob, Plate V, 1.

Plate VI, fig. 17. This terminal is of uncertain origin, but was perhaps made at Leeds or Liverpool, *c.* 1775–80.

Plate VI, fig. 18. This terminal occurs on Leeds creamware and tortoiseshell ware (6) in conjunction with the flower knob Plate V, fig. 5, *c.* 1775–85.

Plate VI, fig. 19. This terminal occurs on some Leeds creamware made before 1775, but may occur on Cockpit Hill, Derby, pieces as well.

Plate VI, 20. This terminal is of uncertain origin, but occurs on very fine quality creamware enamelled by D. Rhodes, and is probably therefore of either Leeds or Wedgwood origin.

---

(1) *Plate* 62A;　(2) *Plates* 31A, 32, 36, 38; (3) *Plate* 31B; (4) *Plates* 13B, 34B; (5) *Plate* 35A, B; (6) *Plate* 37.

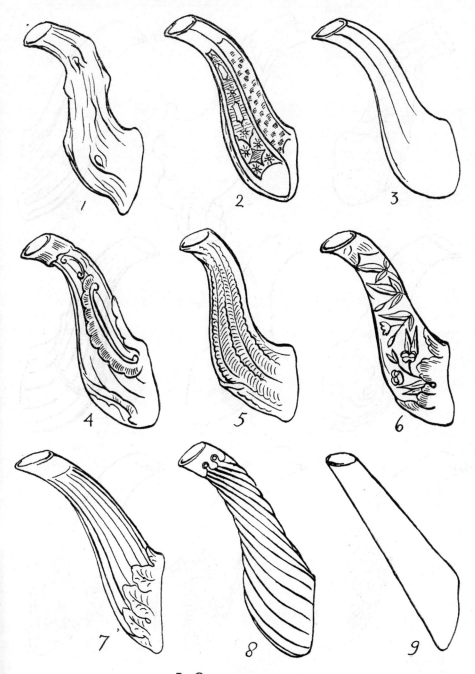

I. Creamware spouts

See pages 64 and 65

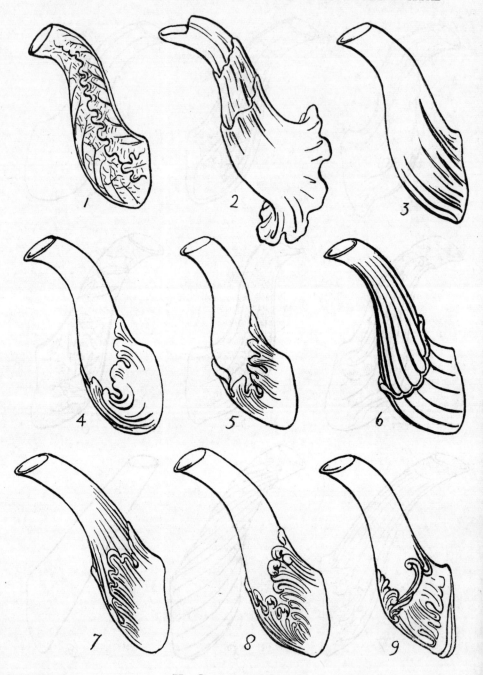

II. Creamware spouts

See pages 65 and 66

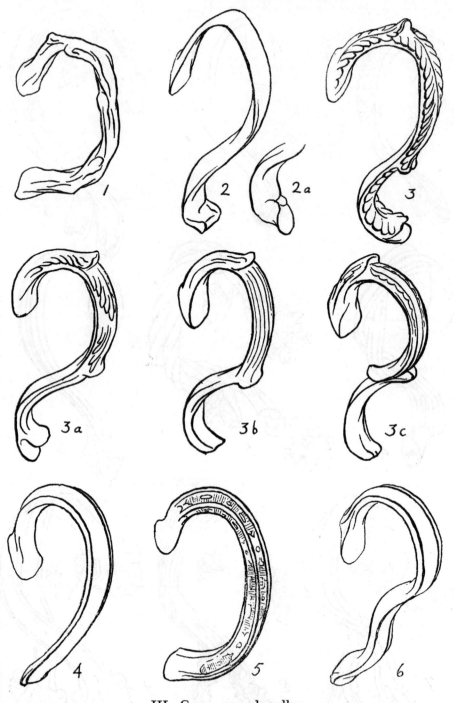

III. Creamware handles

See pages 67 and 68

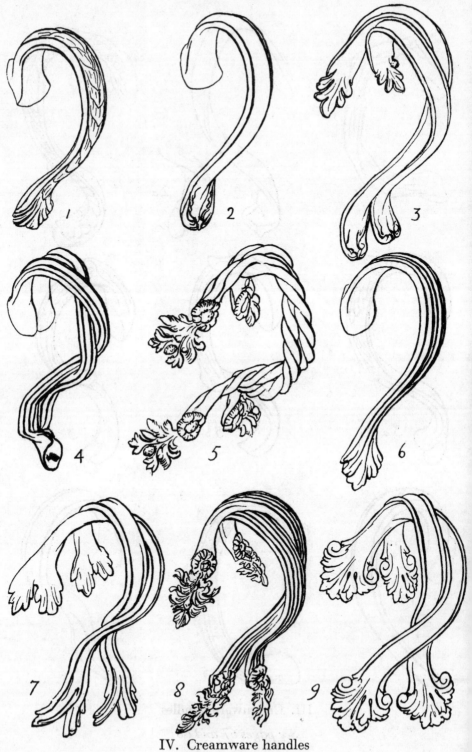

IV. Creamware handles

See pages 68 and 69

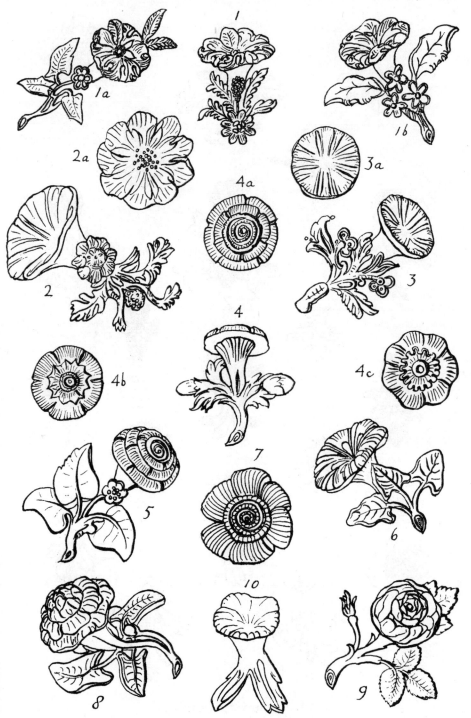

V. Creamware flower knobs

See pages 70 and 71

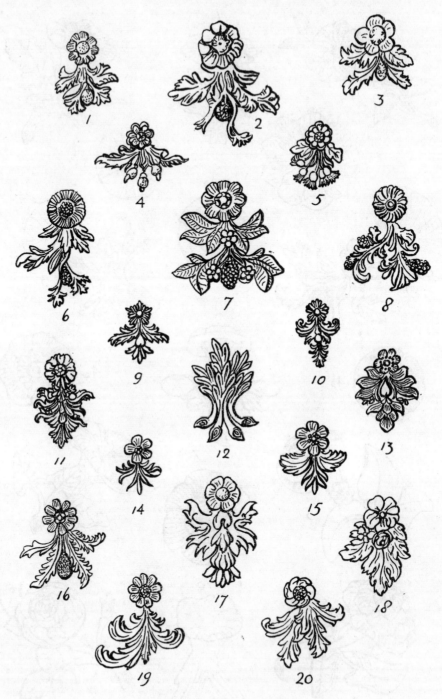

VI. Creamware terminals

See pages 71 and 72

Appendix II

PATTERN AND DRAWING BOOKS

THE LEEDS POTTERY PATTERN AND DRAWING BOOKS
(see page 24)

Plates VII and VIII show tracings of engravings from the Leeds Pattern Book. Plate IX, shows tracings of drawings from the Leeds Drawing Books. These plates do not correspond to actual plates in the pattern and drawing books, but consist of groupings of selected examples.

Pattern books were issued by the Leeds pottery in the years 1783, 1785, 1786, 1794 and 1814.[1] The title page of the first pattern book bears the following inscription:

'Designs of Sundry Articles of Queen's or Cream Colour'd Earthenware manufacture by Hartley, Greens & Co., at Leeds Pottery with a great variety of other Articles. The same Enamell'd, Printed or Ornamented with gold to any pattern; also with Coats of Arms, Cyphers, Landscapes, etc. etc. Leeds 1783.'

The pattern books contain plates with engraved illustrations. A list describing the plates was issued under separate cover. This list which is now very rare is reproduced in J. and F. Kidson, *Historical Notices of the Leeds Old Pottery*, Leeds, 1892. The 1783 edition contains forty plates, the articles being numbered from 1 to 152 followed by 1 to 32 for tea ware. The subsequent editions contain 31 new plates in addition, the new designs being numbered from 153 to 212, and 33 to 48 for tea ware.

There are three drawing books at the Victoria and Albert Museum entitled 'Original Drawing Book No. 1': 'Original Drawing Book No. 2': 'New Teapot Book.' These consist of drawings and designs pasted into old account books of the Leeds Pottery. Some of the accounts are still visible, but are for the most part difficult to decipher. The following entries, however, occur frequently: 'Ordered at Swinton, to be marked etc.': 'Ordered from Swinton to come here.' These show the close connection between these two Yorkshire potteries and indicate that at least some of the marked pieces were destined for the Swinton Pottery. These drawing books date from about 1778 to 1792. The date 1778 occurs on the drawing of a mug with a scroll handle (Plate IX).

[1] The 1814 edition is undated, but the date may be seen in the watermark of the paper.

The 'New Teapot Book' though undated seems to date from about 1790 to about 1820. The designs which are in colour include the following patterns:

Green-glazed vertical bands (see page 20).
Reeded horizontal bands filled in with green glaze.
Underglaze blue pagoda patterns.
Enamelled sprays of flowers in red, black and green.
Enamelled 'Chinaman in a garden' pattern.
Cloudy and mottled glazes (see page 19).
Granite wares.
Cream-colour banded with deep orange-buff (see page 24).
Bright blue ground with small chequered borders of black and white (see page 24).
Many formal patterns in mineral colours of brown, buff, sage-green and a soft deep blue (see page 23).
A large number of border patterns resembling those painted for Wedgwood at his Chelsea workshops (see page 24).
Landscapes, and a series copied from Thomas Bewick's wood-engravings.

The following drawing books are in the Leeds City Museum and Art Gallery:

Drawing Book No. 1 dated 1781. Although this book is labelled No. 1 it is unlikely that it is the first as the drawings contained in it are numbered from 153 to 231.
Drawing Book No. 2 dated 1803. The drawings numbered from 274 to 375.
Drawing Book No. 3 dated 1814, drawings numbered 401 to 457.
Drawing Book No. 4. No doubt the last, as it is undated and the drawings unnumbered.
Handle Drawing Book.
Black Ware (Basalt) Drawing Book dated 1800.
Enamel Tea Service Book (in colour).
Enamel Tea Ware (in colour).
Ornamental Drawing Book No. 1 dated 1801.

The first four of these books contain many of the original drawings from which the engravings were made for the pattern books, as references beside the drawings show.

THE WEDGWOOD CREAMWARE PATTERN BOOKS
(see page 42)

Wedgwood's 'First Pattern Book', which is now at the Wedgwood

Museum, Barlaston, was begun about 1770. This book contained drawings for use within the factory and was not published. Additions to the book were made continuously until the year 1814. Included among the designs are patterns in colour for the borders of the early Queen's ware.

In 1774, Wedgwood first published a creamware pattern book. This was entitled 'A Catalogue of the different Articles of *Queen's Ware*, which may be had either plain, gilt, or embellished with Enamel Paintings, manufactured by Josiah Wedgwood, Potter to her Majesty.' This pattern book consisted of nine engraved plates which depicted thirty-five different articles of creamware. A descriptive list of these articles was issued on a separate sheet and both the list and the book of engravings were sent out together in boxes which also contained actual specimens of creamware.[1] This pattern book is of great rarity but is reproduced in Harry Barnard, *Chats on Wedgwood*, London, 1924, without the list; and in full, together with the list, in Jean Gorely, *Old Wedgwood*, Wellesley, Mass., 1942.

If the designs contained in the Wedgwood and Leeds pattern books be compared the differences of design between the wares of the two factories will, in most cases, be strikingly apparent.

In 1774, Thomas Bentley prepared a catalogue of the famous creamware service, made for the Empress Catherine II of Russia, which consisted of nearly a thousand pieces. The title of the catalogue reads: 'Catalogue and General Description of a Complete Service of Porcelain or Queen's China Ornamented with Various Views of Ruins in Great Britain, Country Seats of the Nobility, Gardens, Landscapes and other Embellishments, All painted in Enamel & Executed According to the Orders and Instructions of the Most Illustrious Patroness of Arts the Empress of all the Russians, By Her Imperial Majesty's Very Humble and Most Grateful Servants Wedgwood and Bentley, London, 1774.'

Two further books of Queen's ware, known as 'Shape Books' were produced in 1803 and in 1817 for use within the factory. The illustrations for the 1817 shape book were engraved by John Taylor Wedgwood and William Blake the artist and poet, and consists of patterns for table, kitchen and dairy ware (1). This book also contains designs in colour for border patterns.

In addition to the creamware catalogues, Wedgwood published a number of catalogues of ornamental stoneware.

---

[1] A version of this pattern book and list, written in French, and containing thirteen plates of engraved designs, is at the Wedgwood Museum, Barlaston.

(1) *Plate* 90A.

ENGLISH CREAM-COLOURED EARTHENWARE

THE CASTLEFORD POTTERY PATTERN BOOK (see page 45)

A copy of this book in the Victoria and Albert Museum is written in both French and Spanish. It contains 57 plates and 259 engraved designs. Many of these show considerable differences of design from the Leeds patterns. The title page has the following inscription: 'Desseins des pièces de Fayence fabriquées à Castleford Pottery près de Leeds par Dᵈ Dunderdale & Co. 1796.' From this pattern book it is apparent that although the double intertwined handle was a usual feature of the creamware of the Castleford Pottery, it generally ended in a foliate shape and neither the applied terminals, which were such a feature of the handles made by the Leeds Pottery, nor the flower knob, seem to have been made at Castleford to any extent. The usual forms of knob made by this factory seems to have been a simple flattened-ball knob and a knob shaped like an onion. Knobs shaped as fruit were also used.

VII. Tracings from the Leeds Pattern Book
'68, Melon Terrine and Spoon. 16, Shell Edge Sauce Boat. 25, Square Chocolate. 26, Common Chocolate. 27, Handled Tea Cup. A, the Saucer for ditto. 65, Plain Cover'd Mug.'

See page 79

VIII. Tracings from the Leeds Pattern Book
'20, Plain handled Sugar Cup. 2, Plain Square Tea Pot. 4, Round Plain
ditto. 10, Square Cannister. 12, Fluted Milk Pot. 6, Plain Coffee Pot.'

See page 79

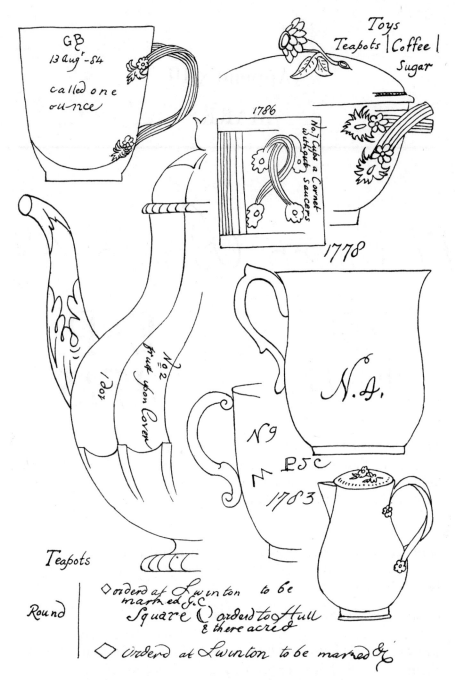

GB
13 aug^t -84

called one
ounce

Toys
Teapots | Coffee |
Sugar

1786

No 1 Cups a Cornet
without Saucers

1778

1 oz

No 2
Knob upon Cover

N.A.

N 9

P 5 C
1783

M

Teapots

Round

◇ orderd at Swinton   to be
marked J. C
Square ◯ ordered to Hull
& there acred

◇ orderd at Swinton to be marked Of

IX. Tracings from Leeds Drawing Books

See pages 79 and 80

Appendix III
MARKS

1

17 Enoch Booth 42

2

1750

E B

3

E×B

J743

Enoch Booth of Tunstall, Staffordshire (see page 5)

1. Incised and filled in with cobalt blue on the front of a scratch-blue saltglaze mug at the Fitzwilliam Museum, Cambridge (see Bernard Rackham, *Early Staffordshire Pottery*, London, 1951, Plate 54).

2. Incised and filled in with cobalt blue on the front of a scratch-blue loving-cup, at the Hanley Museum (see J. C. Wedgwood, *Staffordshire Potters*, London, 1914, Plate facing page 68).

3. Painted in underglaze blue, beneath a creamware bowl at the British Museum (1).

Cockpit Hill, Derby (see pages 10–14)

4 and 5. Transfer-printed in black by Thomas Radford on a creamware teapot at the British Museum (2). These and other variations, for example 'T. Radford Sc. Derby', are the marks of the engraver Thomas Radford and are sometimes found on transfer-printed specimens of Cockpit Hill creamware.

---

(1) *Plates* 1A, B, 2A; (2) *Plate* 11A, B.

4

Radford ſc. DERBy Pot Works

5

Pot Works in DERBY ⚓ *Derby* 6

6. Transfer printed in black on Cockpit Hill creamware (1). The anchor mark is usually ascribed to Richard Holdship (rebus for holdship) (see footnote on page 11).

The *Leeds Pottery* (see pages 15–25)

7. Impressed. Length $1\frac{1}{8}$ in.[1] This is probably the first mark to be used by the Leeds Pottery, and occurs on a shell sweet-meat dish of a deep cream-colour, made before 1775, in the author's collection (2). The different style of lettering to the later marks should be noted.

8 to 11. Impressed. These are the usual marks which occur on Leeds creamware made after 1775 and approximately before 1790. These marks vary in length from $1\frac{1}{8}$ in. to $1\frac{1}{4}$ in. The asterisk, full-stop and hyphen are used in varying positions, but their significance is not known. The set-up of the letters is not mechanically exact; the mark is often slightly curved. Numerals impressed in larger type refer to sizes.

12. Impressed. Length, $1\frac{1}{4}$ in. This mark which is in a different type was used by the Leeds Pottery about 1790 (3).

13. Impressed. Length, $1\frac{1}{8}$ in. This mark usually occurs on Leeds Pottery figures made approximately between 1780 and 1800. The type is slightly irregular and it is sometimes impressed twice on a single piece (4).

14. Impressed. Length 1 in. or less. This mark, in which the type is compressed, is believed to have been used by another factory working at Leeds, and is not the mark of the original factory. Creamware with this mark is often decorated in underglaze-blue painting. It also occurs on some figures of horses (see page 24). Such pieces would appear to have been made between approximately 1800 and 1830.

[1] Measurements are taken in each case between the left-hand serif of the L and the right-hand serif of the Y or to the punctuation mark beyond the Y if such exists, but does not include any numeral following.

(1) *Plate* 10A, B; (2) *Plate* 27A; (3) *Plate* 42B; (4) *Plates* 56, 57, 58, 59.

7
LEEDS·POTTERY

8
LEEDS * POTTERY.
3

9
LEEDS·POTTERY 2

10
LEEDS POTTERY•

11
LEEDS POTTERY—

12
LEEDS * POTTERY.

13
LEEDS POTTERY.

14
LEEDS — POTTERY

15
LEEDS.POTTERY

16
HARTLEY GREENS & Co.
LEEDS * POTTERY

17
Leeds Pottery.

18
HARTLEY GREENS & Cº
LEEDS * POTTERY

19
LEEDS * POTTERY.
LEEDS * POTTERY.

20
HARTLEY·GREENS·&·Cº
LEEDS·POTTERY

21
HARTLEY·GREENS·&·Cº
LEEDS·GREENS·&·Cº
HARTLEY·POTTERY

22
LP

23
G

24
R.B. & S.

25
L

26
HM

27
♠

28
☽

29
L

30
4

31
V

32
Wood
O
1803

33
BJ

34
Samuel
Bawl
1769

35
GREEN, LEEDS,
1768

36
X

37
LEEDS POTTERY

15. Impressed. Length 1 in. The type is straight and regular. This mark was used at the Leeds Pottery on creamware from approximately 1800 till 1820. It also occurs on creamware of more recent date. Some pieces with this mark have the year 1915 impressed on them, and were sold during the 1914–18 war in aid of Queen Alexandra's Red Cross fund. Such pieces differ considerably from the original creamware of the old pottery. Over elaboration of pierced decoration is usual (1); the glaze is more glassy and differs in colour from the original glazes; the crazing on such pieces is of a different character to that on the original creamware and sometimes covers the entire piece; the modelling is less sharp and the general appearance often looks dirty and lacks the brilliance and the life of the original ware.

16, 18, 19, 20 and 21. Impressed. These marks were used by the Leeds Pottery on creamware made after about 1800.

17. Transfer-printed. This mark occurs on some of the engravings made at the Leeds Pottery for transfer-printing upon creamware (2). Some transfer-printed pieces having this mark are also impressed with one of the impressed marks 8 to 11 or mark 22.

22. Impressed or enamelled. This mark impressed is a factory mark of the Leeds Pottery dating from approximately 1780 till 1820. The letters LP enamelled in blue occur on one corner of the saddle-cloth of a figure of a horse about 16 in. high at the Yorkshire Museum, and it is probable that this is not a mark of the original Leeds Pottery but of another pottery working at Leeds during the early years of the nineteenth century (see page 24).

23. Impressed. This mark is occasionally found on creamware made at the Leeds Pottery towards the end of the eighteenth century. Though it may stand for 'Green', it is more probably a workman's mark.

24. Transfer-printed in blue or other colours (quoted by Kidson). This was probably the last mark to be used by the Leeds Pottery and was the mark of Richard Britton & Son, 1872–78.

25. Incised. This mark occurs on a candelabrum at the Victoria and Albert Museum. This piece consists of an urn-shaped vase with winged female figures on either side. Metal branched candle-holders were originally inserted between the wings. It is illustrated in the original pattern book of the Leeds Pottery No. 116 and in J. and F. Kidson, *Historical Notices of the Leeds Old Pottery*, Leeds, 1892, Plate 15. Some very close copies of this piece were made on the Continent. As the mark consists of the letters 'LP' combined in a

---

(1) *Plate* 69; (2) *Plates* 60, 61.

monogram, it may be a factory mark, but no other example is at present known.

26. Impressed. This mark is sometimes found stamped underneath the covers of teapots, coffee-pots, tea-caddies, covered-jugs, etc. (1). These pieces show the finest quality of potting, material and work-manship, and are decorated with flowers painted in crimson enamel. The terminals to the double intertwined handles and flower knob are touched with green. There is little doubt that pieces with this mark are all from one service and were made by the Leeds Pottery, though it is tempting to assign them to the neighbouring pottery at Holbeck Moor, which is reputed to have made a fine quality creamware in the eighteenth century (see page 45). This service has been erroneously ascribed to the factory at Temple Back, Bristol, but a mark of that factory was 'MH', not 'HM' (see page 57).

27. Impressed, occurs on some pieces of Leeds creamware. An impressed 'spade' mark also occurs on some creamware made at the Swansea factory.

28. Impressed. This mark was sometimes impressed on Leeds creamware of an early date (2). It also occurs on moulds from the original Leeds Pottery, which are now at Temple Newsam House, Leeds.

29. Impressed. A large centre-piece of a slightly grey colour, at the Leeds City Art Gallery is impressed with this mark. The probable date of this piece is c. 1860. Kidson quotes this mark as being used at the Leeds Pottery during the period of Richard Britton's ownership (1853–78).

30. Incised, on some deep cream-coloured ware made at Leeds before 1775 (3).

31. Incised. This mark occurs in conjunction with the impressed mark 'LEEDS * POTTERY', on pieces of creamware, green-glazed ware and tortoiseshell ware. It is very doubtful whether such pieces are the products of the original Leeds Pottery.

32. Incised, in conjunction with the Leeds Pottery mark No. 8, impressed twice on a pearlware puzzle-jug at the Leeds City Art Gallery (see Donald Towner, *Handbook of Leeds Pottery*, Leeds, 1951, No. 90). The name 'WOOD' incised in similar hand-writing also occurs on some pearlware oval-shaped teapots enamelled in colours, which were made about 1800.

33. Incised; these marks occur on a mould for sauce-boats from the original Leeds Pottery and now at Temple Newsam House, Leeds. The impressed crescent combined with a large incised letter 'B' and

---

(1) *Plate* 33; (2) *Plates* 22B, 23A; (3) Plate 26B.

other marks which are undecipherable occur on a teapot owned by
Mrs. H. McLeod (1).

34. Incised on a deep cream-coloured screw-top box of Leeds origin
at the Fitzwilliam Museum, Cambridge (2).

35. Incised, on a creamware plaque fitted into the base of a Wedgwood creamware coffee-pot, at the Leeds City Art Gallery. No such
mark was used by the Leeds Pottery.

36. Incised. This mark occurs in conjunction with the Leeds Pottery impressed mark No. 8, but is also found on Wedgwood
creamware.

37. Impressed. Length $\frac{7}{8}$ in. The mark 'LEEDS POTTERY' without
any punctuation marks, mostly occurs on cream-coloured ware of
recent manufacture some of which is semi translucent. But a small
dish with a pierced openwork centre, at the Victoria and Albert
Museum, is impressed with this mark, and was undoubtedly made by
the original Leeds Pottery *c.* 1805.

38

Greatbatch

39

Published as the Act directs Jan.y 4 1778 by W. Greatbatch Lane-Delf Staffordshire.

William Greatbatch, engraver, Lane-Delph, Staffordshire (see pages
26–32)

38 and 39 (3). Transfer-printed in black. These marks sometimes
occur on creamware teapots, which are transfer-printed in black and
coloured over in enamels, and should be taken as applying to the engravings only (see page 30).

Josiah Wedgwood (see pages 33–42)

40 to 46. Impressed. There were many slight variations of type and
spacing in the Wedgwood marks on creamware made before *c.* 1775,
which is exemplified by the marks 40 to 46. Some of these, will be
seen to be in lower-case letters beginning with a small 'w', others are
in lower-case letters beginning with a large 'W'. Some are in capital
letters, but all are irregularly spaced. These marks were often used in

---

(1) *Plate* 22B; (2) *Plate* 26A; (3) *Plate* 66B.

40
wedgwood

41
Wedgwood

42
wedgwood

43
Wedgwood

44
WEDGWOOD

45
WEDGWOOD

46
WEDGWOOD

47
WEDGWOOD

48
Wedgwood

49
WEDGWOOD

50
WEDGWOOD.

51
WEDGWOOD
ADR

52
WEDGWOOD
ETRURIA

53
Pearl

54
WEDGWOOD
ENGLAND

55 *B*

56 *g*

57 OF ETRURIA WEDGWOOD & BARLASTON MADE IN ENGLAND

58 V

59 B

60 ◯

61 C

62 ♡

63 ⛊

64 ✻

65 O

66 ⬭

67 ◯

68 𝒮𝓌

69 ▢

70 ◇

71 ∷

72 ⊏

73 ◡

74 ⦀⦀

75 W

76 ⋁

77 𝕬

78 ‖

79 ⏝

80 ◇

81 C

82 ✕

83 ✓

84 h

92

conjunction with workmen's marks. The pieces illustrated in this book on which the marks 40 to 46 occur are shown on the following plates:

40. (combined with 61), Plate 79*b*.
41. (combined with 78), Plate 87*a*.
42. Plate 84.
43. (combined with 60), Plate 76*b*.
44. Plate 83*a*.
45. (combined with 64), Plate 85.
46. (combined with 56), Plate 86*a*.

47 and 48. Impressed. These are the first regular marks. 47 has the 'O's widely spaced and oval in shape, 48 is in lower-case letters. They seem to have been used on creamware made between approximately 1770 and 1775.

49. Impressed. This was the mark extensively used by the Wedgwood factory from about 1775 to the present day.

50. Impressed. This mark is sometimes found impressed on the back of figures made to Wedgwood's order by the Wood family at Burslem (see pages 42, 51). The mark from which the illustration was taken occurs on a large creamware bust at the Victoria and Albert Museum by Enoch Wood. The word 'SADNESS' is impressed on the front. The mark No. 50 varies in size according to the size of the figure upon which it is impressed. The irregularities of the letters themselves also vary slightly.

51. Impressed. The Wedgwood mark used in conjunction with three letters (of which mark 51 is an example) was introduced in 1860. The first letter indicates the month, the second letter indicates the potter's initial or mark, and the third letter, the year in which the piece was made. The sequence of letters, standing for the year began with the letter O for 1860 and continued in sequence through the alphabet to Z for 1871 and then began with A for 1872 and continued through the entire alphabet to Z for 1897. The year 1898 was indicated by A, and the cycle was repeated, Z standing for 1923.[1]

52. Impressed. The letters of this mark will be seen to be more widely spaced than the normal mark. It was impressed on white-ware made about 1840. Such ware is usually very light in weight.

53. Impressed on some pieces of pearlware from *c.* 1780.

54. Impressed. The word 'ENGLAND' was added to the normal mark in 1891.

55 and 56. Enamelled. These marks frequently occur under pieces

---

[1] A complete list of date marks, which includes the month as well as the year, is set out in Josiah Wedgwood & Sons, catalogue of *Early Wedgwood Pottery* (exhibited at 34 Wigmore Street, London), Burslem. 1951.

of deep cream-coloured dessert services. Such pieces are usually painted with flowers in purple or crimson (1) and are sometimes impressed with the Mark 46, as well. Marks 55 and 56 were enamellers' marks, the letter 'B' standing for Bakewell (see pages 38, 39).

57. Printed in colour. This mark was introduced in 1940, and is used on the present-day creamware made by Josiah Wedgwood & Sons, Barlaston.

58 and 59. Impressed potter's marks. These two marks are of frequent occurrence on Wedgwood creamware made during the eighteenth century.

60 and 61. Impressed potter's marks. These marks are sometimes found in conjunction with the early impressed factory marks and were in use before 1775. The teapot on Plate 76*b* is impressed with marks 60 and 43, that on Plate 79*b*, with marks 61 and 40.

62 and 63. Impressed potter's marks. 62 combined with 48 and 67 is impressed on the cake-basket illustrated on Plate 91*a*; 63 combined with 42 is impressed on the covered jug shown on Plate 84.

64. Impressed potter's mark. This mark used in conjunction with 45 is impressed under the coffee-pot shown on Plate 85.

65. Impressed potter's mark. This little mark is of frequent occurrence on Wedgwood's eighteenth-century creamware. It is sometimes found impressed under the covers of teapots and coffee-pots. It is impressed on the coffee-pot shown on Plate 81.

66. Impressed potter's mark, which is sometimes combined with the normal impressed factory mark.

67. Turned. A circular mark formed by a tool in the centre of the base of a piece of creamware while it was being turned, is of frequent occurrence on the wares of both the Wedgwood and Leeds factories.

68. Incised. These letters which almost certainly stand for Josiah Wedgwood, occur on the base of a cauliflower-ware tea-caddy in the Victoria and Albert Museum. The caddy is not creamware in the strict sense of the word but of a common earthenware. It is possible that the initials are those of John Wedgwood, John Warburton, or Jacob Warburton, but the style of letters exactly corresponds with Josiah Wedgwood's handwriting.

69 to 74. Impressed potter's marks which sometimes occur in conjunction with the normal Wedgwood impressed factory mark on eighteenth century creamware.

75 and 76. Incised. These are undoubtedly two of the earliest potter's marks to be found on Wedgwood's creamware. 75 occurs in

(1) *Plate* 86A.

conjunction with 42 on the covered-jug illustrated on Plate 84. These marks would appear to date from about 1765.

77, 79, 80 and 81. Impressed, eighteenth-century potter's marks on Wedgwood's creamware.

78, 83 and 84. Incised, eighteenth-century potter's marks on Wedgwood's creamware.

82. Incised. This mark occurs on the eighteenth-century creamware of both the Wedgwood and Leeds factories.

In addition to Marks 40 to 82, which occur on Wedgwood's creamware, a circular stamp containing the words 'WEDGWOOD AND BENTLEY ETRURIA' is sometimes found on the stoneware base of creamware vases made in imitation of stones (see page 41). This mark never occurs on creamware itself.

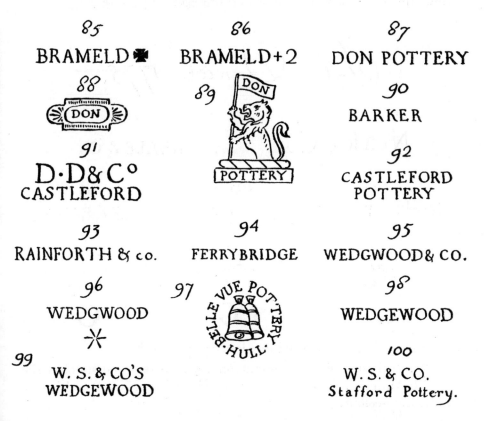

Swinton and the Later Yorkshire Potteries (see pages 43–46)

85 and 86. Impressed on creamware and green glazed ware, are marks of the Swinton Pottery (see page 43). L. Jewitt in *Ceramic Art of Great Britain*, London, 1883, quotes Mark 85 followed by an additional cross. The impressed mark 'BRAMELD' in capital letters without

any additions is quoted by A. Hurst in *A Catalogue of the Boynton Collection of Yorkshire Pottery*, York, 1922.

87 to 90. Impressed, are the marks of the Don Pottery at Swinton (see page 44).

91 and 92. Impressed, are marks of the Castleford Pottery (see page 45).

93. Impressed. This mark was used after 1792 at Petty's Pottery, Holbeck Moor (see page 45).

94 and 95. Impressed, are the marks of the Ferrybridge and Knottingley Potteries (see page 45).

96, 98, 99 and 100. Impressed, are the marks of the Stafford Pottery, Stockton-on-Tees (see page 46).

97. Impressed, is the mark of the Belle Vue Pottery at Hull. Sometimes the lettering is omitted from this mark (see page 46).

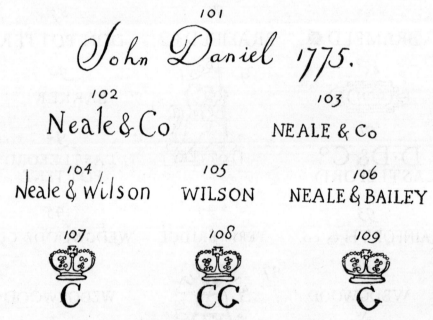

John Daniel of Cobridge and Burslem (see page 9)

101. Incised. This mark occurs on a cake-basket and stand at the British Museum. It is decorated with pierced open-work and is of a rich cream-colour.

Neale & Co. Hanley (see pages 47–48)

102 (1) and 103 (2). Impressed marks used by this factory before 1786.

---

(1) *Plate* 94A (No. 1), B (No. 1, 2); (2) *Plate* 95A.

110

R.WOOD

111

79

Ra.Wood

Burslem

112

114

E.WOOD

113

W (✳ ✳ ✳)

115

ENOCH WOOD

116

WOOD & CALDWELL

117

E·MAYER

118

E. Mayer

119

Adams & Co

120

ADAMS

121

TURNER

122

SPODE

123

SPODE

124

DAVENPORT

125

Davenport

126

J. Aynsley Lane End

127

SHORTHOSE

128

Shorthose & Co

129

WARBURTON

130

P&F. WARBURTON.

131

P&F. Warburton.

104, 105 and 106. Impressed marks used by this factory after 1786.

107, 108 and 109. Impressed. These marks were used by Wilson who was John Neale's partner from 1786. They are sometimes erroneously stated to have been used by the Leeds Pottery.

The Wood family of Burslem (see pages 50, 51)

110, 111 and 112. Impressed. These are the factory marks of Ralph Wood of Burslem, senior and junior. 112 which is stamped in low relief, is a rebus for 'Wood'. This and 110 are sometimes to be found on the earlier figures and may therefore be the marks of Ralph Wood, senior; whereas 111 occurs on the later figures and may be considered the mark of Ralph Wood, junior.

113. Impressed. This is almost certainly a mark of Enoch Wood.

114 and 115. Impressed, are also marks of Enoch Wood, and were probably used between 1783 and 1790.

H

116. Impressed. The partnership mark of Enoch Wood and James Caldwell, which was used between 1790 and 1819.

Elijah Mayer of Hanley (see page 49)
117 and 118. Impressed marks.

William Adams of Greengates, Tunstall (see page 52)
119 and 120. Impressed marks.

John Turner of Lane End (see page 48)
121. Impressed mark (1).

Josiah Spode of Stoke (see page 52)
122 and 123. Impressed marks.

John Davenport of Longport (see page 52)
124 and 125. Impressed marks.

John Aynsley of Lane End (see page 49)
126. Transfer-printed. John Aynsley was an engraver. It should not be assumed that he manufactured the ware on which this mark occurs.

Shorthose and Heath of Hanley (see page 51)
127 and 128. Impressed mark.

Peter and Francis Warburton of Cobridge (see page 9)
129, 130 and 131. Impressed. Marks 130 and 131 occur on cream-ware figures, and some cruets which have a central figure. Such pieces are of the finest quality. Mark 129 occurs on white-ware vases in the neo-classical style, which may have been made by another branch of the family.

Liverpool, Bristol, Swansea and other marks (see pages 54–58)
132 and 133 (2). Transfer-printed. These are marks of Sadler and Green, a firm of printers at Liverpool who were responsible for most of the printing on Wedgwood's creamware (see page 54).
134 (3), 135 and 136. Transfer-printed. These are the marks of Richard Abbey who engraved for Sadler and Green in the first place but started business on his own account in 1773. These marks probably date from this time (see page 55). Mark 136 occurs on a teapot at the Castle Museum, Norwich, made by Joseph Johnson of Liverpool.

---

(1) *Plate* 96A; (2) *Plate* 83B; (3) *Plate* 93B.

132

J. Sadler Liverpool

133

Green, Liverpool

134

Abbey, Liverpool

135

R. Abbey, sculp

136

Rd. Abbey, Sculp

137

Johnson

138

Josh. Johnson Liverpool

139

Billinge sculptor Liverpool

140

HERCULANEUM

141

SEWELLS & DONKIN
D

142

SEWELL & DONKIN

143

SEWELL

144

ST. ANTHONY'S

145

FELL

146

T. FELL & Co.

147

FELL
NEWCASTLE

148

PHILLIPS & CO.

149

DIXON & Co.
Sunderland Pottery

150

DIXON AUSTIN & Co.

151

MOORE & Co. Southwick.

152

SWANSEA

153

DILLWYN & COM.
10

154

DILLWYN & Co

158

Bristol Pottery

155   157   156

S   Ω   C

159

J. Eaves   Bristol

160

Absolon Yarm

161

Y

162

Absolon yarm N25

137 and 138. Transfer-printed. Joseph Johnson of Liverpool appears to have been both an engraver and a potter (see under Mark 136); the mark, in most cases, probably relates to the engraving only.

139. Transfer-printed. The mark of Thomas Billinge, engraver of Liverpool (see page 55).

140. Impressed. The mark of the Herculaneum factory at Toxteth Park, Liverpool (see page 55).

141, 142, 143 and 144. Impressed, are the factory marks of Sewell and Donkin of the St. Anthony's Pottery, Newcastle-upon-Tyne (see page 56).

145, 146 and 147. Impressed, are the factory marks of Thomas Fell of the St. Peter's Pottery, Newcastle-upon-Tyne (see page 56).

148, 149 and 150. Impressed, are the marks of Dixon, Austin, Phillips & Co. who worked a pottery at Sunderland. They produced a coarse white-ware decorated with lustre, transfer-prints, etc., which cannot be considered creamware except in the very widest sense (see page 56).

151. Transfer-printed, on some of the ware made at the Southwick Pottery on the River Wear. This pottery was founded in 1788 by Anthony Scott, who produced a coarse white-ware with transfer-printed and lustre decoration, which cannot be considered creamware, except in the very widest sense.

152, 153 and 154. Impressed. Factory marks of L. W. Dillwyn at Swansea (see page 57).

155 and 156. Impressed. Factory marks of the Swansea factory (see page 57. Mark 155 was sometimes painted in red enamel).

157. Impressed. A potter's mark of the Swansea factory (see page 57).

158. Transfer-printed. This mark occurs on some transfer-printed ware made at Joseph's Ring's factory at Temple Back, Bristol, *c.* 1802 (1) (see page 57).

159. Enamelled. The mark of an enameller at Joseph Ring's factory, Bristol (see page 57).

160, 161, 162. Enamelled. These marks occur on creamware made by Davenport, Turner and at other factories. They were the marks of Absolon, an independent enameller at Yarmouth (see page 49).

---

(1) *Plate* 96B (No. 1).

BIBLIOGRAPHY

Simeon Shaw, *History of the Staffordshire Potteries*, Hanley, 1829.

Eliza Meteyard, *The Life of Josiah Wedgwood*, London, 1865.

Llewellyn Jewitt, *Ceramic Art of Great Britain*, London, 1878.

Joseph and Frank Kidson, *Historical Notices of the Leeds Old Pottery*, Leeds, 1892.

Maud Sellers, *Pottery, A History of the County of York* (Victoria County Histories, Vol. II, 1912).

J. C. Wedgwood, *Staffordshire Pottery and its History*, London, 1914.

Oxley Grabham, *Yorkshire Potteries, Pots and Potters*, York, 1916.

W. J. Pountney, *The Old Bristol Potteries*, London and Bristol, 1920.

Arthur Hurst, *Catalogue of the Boynton Collection of Yorkshire Pottery*, York, 1922.

Emil Hannover, *Pottery and Porcelain* (translated from the Danish by Bernard Rackham), London, 1925.

Bernard Rackham, *Catalogue of the Schreiber Collection*, Vol. II, London, 1929.

F. Williamson, *The Derby Pot-Manufactory known as Cockpit Hill*, Derby, 1931.

Bernard Rackham, *Catalogue of the Glaisher Collection* (Fitzwilliam Museum, Cambridge), Cambridge, 1934.

W. B. Honey, *Wedgwood Ware*, London, 1948.

E. Stanley Price, *John Sadler a Liverpool Pottery Printer*, West Kirby, 1948.

Bernard Rackham, *Early Staffordshire Pottery*, London, 1951.

Donald C. Towner, *Handbook of Leeds Pottery*, Leeds, 1951.

W. B. Honey, *European Ceramic Art*, London, 1952.

Wolf Mankowitz, *Wedgwood*, London, 1953.

Geoffrey Godden, 'Derby Pot Works, Cockpit Hill' in *Transactions of the English Ceramic Circle*, Vol. III, Part IV, 1955.

Donald C. Towner, 'The Leeds Pottery, Jack Lane, Hunslet', in *Transactions of the English Ceramic Circle*, Vol. III, Part IV, 1955.

Donald C. Towner, 'Some Creamware Comparisons', in *Transactions of the English Ceramic Circle*, Vol. IV, Part 3, 1957.

INDEX

103

INDEX

INDEX

THE MONOCHROME PLATES

1A. *Punch-bowl. Panels painted in underglaze blue
reserved on a finely speckled manganese ground.
Diam. 10 in. Enoch Booth 1743.
British Museum. See pages 5, 34, 86*
1B. *Underside of the above punch-bowl*

2A. *Interior of the punch-bowl shown on Plate* 1A, 1B
2B. *Teapot painted in underglaze colours.*
Spout, handle and feet in solid agate.
Height 4¾ *in. Probably Whieldon. Circa* 1740.
Mr. and Mrs. Victor Gollancz. See pages 6, 34

3A. *Punch-bowl with applied reliefs touched with
colours under the glaze. Diam. 10 in.
Perhaps Whieldon. Circa 1750.
Victoria and Albert Museum. See page 2*
3B. *Punch-pot with applied reliefs touched with
colours under the glaze. Perhaps Whieldon.
Height 7 in. Circa 1750.
Victoria and Albert Museum. See page 2*

4. *Coffee-pot with applied reliefs touched with colours
under the glaze. Perhaps Whieldon or Wedgwood.
Height 7½ in. Circa 1755.
Victoria and Albert Museum. See page 2*

5. *Coffee-pot, enamelled in pink, green, red and yellow
by a saltglaze decorator. Perhaps Whieldon or Wedgwood.
Circa 1755. Height 9¾ in. Cf. Plate 4
Mr. and Mrs. Victor Gollancz. See page 8*

6A. *Double tea-caddy clouded with colours under the glaze.*
Probably Whieldon. Circa 1750.
Length 6¼ in.
Fitzwilliam Museum Cambridge. See Page 8
6B. *Double tea-caddy in uncoloured creamware.*
Probably Whieldon. Circa 1750. Length 6¼ in.
Victoria and Albert Museum. See page 8

7A. *Sugar-bowl with applied gilded reliefs on a ground clouded with*
brown manganese under the glaze.
Height 3¼ in. Probably Whieldon. Circa 1750.
Victoria and Albert Museum. See page 8

7B. *Sugar-bowl of uncoloured creamware with applied gilded reliefs.*
Height 3¼ in. Probably Whieldon. Circa 1750.
Donald Towner. See page 8

8A. *Teapot, deep cream, enamelled in red and black.*
A wheatsheaf on the reverse.
Height 4¾ in. Cockpit Hill, Derby. 1761.
British Museum. See pages 14, 64

8B. *Teapot, deep cream, enamelled in red, black and green.*
Height 5¼ in. Cockpit Hill, Derby. Circa 1765.
Donald Towner. See pages 13, 64

9A. *Teapot, deep cream, enamelled in red and black; 'No. 45' on the reverse. Height 4½ in. Cockpit Hill, Derby. Circa 1770. Leeds City Art Gallery and Temple Newsam House. See pages* 14, 64
9B. *Teapot, deep cream, enamelled in red, black and green; flowers on the reverse. Height 4 in. Cockpit Hill, Derby. Circa 1770. Donald Towner. See pages* 14, 65

10A. *Teapot, deep cream, transfer printed in black.*
Mark, 'Derby' and an anchor, in the print.
Height 4½ in. Cockpit Hill, Derby. Circa 1765.
Fitzwilliam Museum, Cambridge. See pages 11, 64, 87
10B. *Teapot, reverse side of 10A*

11A. *Teapot, deep cream, transfer printed in black.*
Mark, 'Pot Works in Derby' in the print.
Height 4 in. Cockpit Hill, Derby. Circa 1765.
British Museum. See pages 11, 64, 86
11B. *Teapot, reverse side of 11A.*
Mark, 'Radford Sculpsit Derby Pot Works' in the print.

12. *Saltglaze jug, painted in enamel colours at Leeds.*
Inscribed, 'Success to Mr. John Calverly of Leeds'.
(Mr. John Calverly was elected Mayor of Leeds in 1773.)
Height 7 in.
British Museum. See page 18

15A. *Saltglaze teapot, painted in enamel colours at Leeds.*
Height $4\frac{3}{4}$ *in. Circa* 1770.
Donald Towner. See page 18
15B. *Creamware teapot, deep cream, enamelled in red, green,*
yellow, blue and black. Height $5\frac{1}{2}$ *in.*
Leeds. Circa 1770.
Mr. and Mrs. Victor Gollancz. See pages 18, 72

14A. *Teapot, deep cream, enamelled in red and black.*
Height 5½ in. Leeds. Circa 1765.
Donald Towner. See pages 17, 19
14B. *Teapot, deep cream, enamelled in red and black;*
flower knob blue and yellow, terminals green;
gilding. Height 4½ in. Leeds. Circa 1770.
Donald Towner. See page 64

15A. *Teapot, deep cream, enamelled in red and black.*
Height 5 in. Leeds. Circa 1770.
Donald Towner. See pages 18, 65, 70
15B. *Teapot, deep cream, enamelled in red, black and dull pink.*
Height 5 in. Leeds. Circa 1770.
Donald Towner. See pages 19, 65

16. *Jug, deep cream, enamelled in red, deep pink,
cobalt blue, blue-green, yellow and black.
Height $6\frac{3}{4}$ in. Leeds or Staffordshire 1766. Cf. Plate 12.
Mr. and Mrs. Victor Gollancz. See page 17*

17. *Jug, deep cream, enamelled in red and black.*
Height 8¼ in. Leeds. Circa 1770.
Donald Towner. See page 19

18A. *Bowl, deep cream, enamelled in red, green and black,*
spots in opaque white. Diam. $5\frac{1}{2}$ *in.*
Leeds. Circa 1760.
Donald Towner.
18B. *Punch-pot, deep cream, enamelled in red.*
Height 6 *in. Probably Leeds. Circa* 1765.
Mr. and Mrs. Victor Gollancz. See page 17

19A. *Bowl, deep cream, enamelled in red, black and green.*
Diam. $5\frac{1}{4}$ in. Leeds. Circa 1770.
Mr. and Mrs. Victor Gollancz. See page 18
19B. *Teapot, deep cream, enamelled in red and black.*
A wheatsheaf on the reverse. Height $5\frac{1}{4}$ in.
Leeds. Circa 1770.
Victoria and Albert Museum. See page 71

20. *Jug, deep cream, enamelled in red and black,
gilded beading. 'BEER' within a cartouche.
Height 7¾ in.
Perhaps Whieldon. Painted at Leeds. Circa 1765.
Donald Towner. See pages 8, 19*

21. *Mug, deep cream, enamelled in red and black.*
Height 5¾. Leeds. Circa 1770.
Victoria and Albert Museum. See page 19

22A. *Teapot, deep cream, enamelled in red, black,*
blue and yellow. Height 5 in. Leeds. Circa 1770.
Mr. and Mrs. Victor Gollancz. See page 65
22B. *Teapot, deep cream, enamelled in red, black and blue.*
Marks, an impressed crescent and incised 'B',
these marks also occur on a mould for a sauce-boat from the
Leeds Pottery.
Height 5¼ in. Leeds. Circa 1770.
Mrs. H. McLeod. See page 90

23A. *Teapot, deep cream, enamelled in red, black and green.*
Mark, an impressed crescent, see Plate 22B.
Height 4½ in. Leeds. Circa 1770.
Victoria and Albert Museum. See page 90
23B. *Teapot, deep cream, enamelled in red, black and green.*
Height 4½ in. Leeds. Circa 1770.
Victoria and Albert Museum

24. *Coffee-pot, deep cream, enamelled in red, black, green, yellow and blue. Height 9¾ in. Leeds. Circa 1770.*
Fitzwilliam Museum, Cambridge. See page 70

25. *Coffee-pot, deep cream, enamelled in red, black and deep pink;
some gilding. Height $9\frac{1}{4}$ in.
Leeds. Painted by a Derby painter. Circa 1770.
Mr. and Mrs. Victor Gollancz. See page 14*

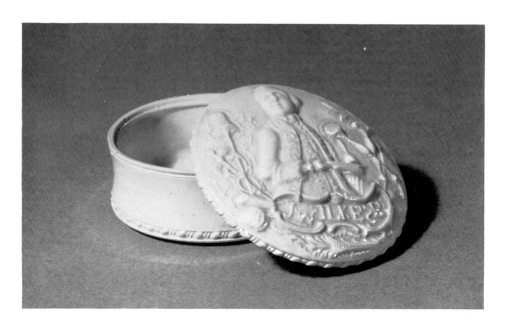

26A. *Box with screw-top, deep cream, uncoloured.*
Mark, 'Samuel Bawl 1769' incised. Diam. 5¼ in.
Leeds. Fitzwilliam Museum, Cambridge. See pages 18, 91
26B. *Punch-pot, deep cream, uncoloured.*
Mark, 'Z' in reverse incised. Height 8½ in. Leeds. Circa 1770.
Donald Towner. See pages 18, 70, 90

27A. *Sweetmeat-dish, deep cream, uncoloured.*
Mark, 'LEEDS * POTTERY', *impressed, length 8 in.*
Circa 1765.
Donald Towner. See pages 16, 87
27B. *Teapot, deep cream, uncoloured. Height* 4½ *in.*
Perhaps Leeds. Circa 1770.
Donald Towner

28. *Coffee-pot, deep cream, uncoloured. Height 9¼ in.*
Leeds. Circa 1770.
Donald Towner. See pages 65, 71

29. *Coffee-pot, deep cream, uncoloured. Height* 10 *in.*
Leeds. Circa 1770.
Donald Towner. See page 71

30A. *Saltglaze teapot, enamelled at Leeds, in*
blue, green, yellow, pink and black.
Buildings on the reverse. Height 4¼ *in.*
Perhaps Leeds. Circa 1770. Cf. Plate 30B, 31A.
Mr. and Mrs. Victor Gollancz. See page 18
30B. *Saltglaze teapot, enamelled as Plate* 30A,
inscribed 'Miss Pit'. Buildings on the reverse. Perhaps Leeds.
Circa 1770. Height 4¼ *in. Cf. Plate* 30A, 31A.
Mr. and Mrs. Victor Gollancz. See page 18

31A. *Creamware teapot, pale cream, enamelled in red.*
Buildings on the reverse. Height 4½ in.
Leeds. Circa 1775. Cf. Plate 30A, 30B.
Donald Towner. See pages 66, 72
31B. *Teapot, pale cream, enamelled in red, green, blue, yellow and*
black. A Chinese figure on the reverse.
Height 6 in. Leeds. Circa 1775.
Donald Towner. See pages 71, 72

32. *Coffee-pot, pale cream, enamelled in red;*
terminals dark red, beading yellow. Height $9\frac{1}{4}$ *in.*
Leeds. Circa 1775. *Cf. Plate* 36.
Donald Towner. See page 72

33. *Coffee-pot, pale cream, enamelled in crimson; terminals green.*
Mark, 'HM' impressed under the cover.
Height 9⅛ in. Leeds, or neighbouring factory. Circa 1775.
Leeds City Art Gallery and Temple Newsam House. See pages 45, 57, 90

34A. *Sugar-bowl, pale cream, enamelled in crimson; terminals green.*
Height 3¼ in. Leeds. Circa 1775.
Donald Towner. See page 70

34B. *Teapot, pale cream, enamelled in purple, crimson, red and green.*
Height 4¼ in. Mark, an incised cross.
Leeds. Circa 1775.
Donald Towner. See pages 66, 72

35A. *Teapot, pale cream, enamelled in dull purple;*
flower knob and terminals in deep green; traces of gilding.
Height 4¾ in. Leeds. Circa 1775.
Donald Towner. See pages 70, 72

35B. *Teapot, pale cream, enamelled in rosy purple,*
red, green, yellow and black; traces of gilding.
Height 4¾ in. Leeds. Circa 1775.
Donald Towner. See pages 70, 72

36. *Coffee-pot, pale cream, uncoloured. Height 8 in.*
Leeds. Circa 1775. Cf. Plates 32, 38.
Mr. and Mrs. Victor Gollancz. See pages 20, 72

57. *Coffee-pot, pale cream, uncoloured. Height* $10\frac{1}{4}$ *in.*
Leeds. Circa 1775. *Cf. Plate* 58.
Donald Towner. See pages 20, 72

38. *Coffee-pot, tortoiseshell ware, mottled with brown manganese.*
Height 9⅞ in. Leeds. Circa 1775. Cf. Plates 36, 37.
Leeds City Art Gallery and Temple Newsam House. See pages 20, 72

39. *Chocolate-pot, tortoiseshell ware,*
mottled with purplish-grey manganese. Height $4\frac{1}{2}$ *in.*
Leeds. Circa 1775.
Victoria and Albert Museum. See page 20

40A. *Tea-cup and saucer, deep cream, enamelled in green.*
Height of cup 1¾ in. Diam. of saucer 4¾ in.
Probably Leeds. Circa 1770.
Donald Towner

40B. *Tea-cup and saucer, pale cream, enamelled in red, purple, green,*
yellow and black. Height of cup 2 in. Diam. of saucer 5 in. Leeds.
Circa 1775.
Donald Towner

41A. *Snuff-boxes as heads, with screw-on bases, pale cream:*
(i) *Decorated with purplish manganese and green underglaze colours;*
(ii) *Enamelled in pink, blue, red, green and yellow;*
(iii) *Enamelled in plum, green, blue, grey and flesh;*
(iv) *Painted in underglaze blue.*
Height 3½ in. Leeds. Circa 1775.
Mr. and Mrs. Victor Gollancz. See page 19
41B. (i) *Mug, pale cream, enamelled in red, pink, green and black.*
Height 2¾ in. probably Staffordshire. Circa 1770;
(ii) *Cream-jug, deep cream, enamelled in red and black, beading in*
cobalt. Height 3 in. Leeds. Circa 1770;
(iii) *Sauceboat (perhaps for cucumber juice), pale cream, enamelled in*
red, black, green and yellow. Height 2 in. Leeds. Circa 1775;
(iv) *Cream-jug, pale cream, enamelled in red and black; terminals*
yellow. Height 3 in. Leeds. Circa 1775.
Donald Towner

42A. *Saltglaze mould for dish, from the Leeds Pottery* $8\frac{1}{2} \times 6\frac{1}{2}$ *in.*
Circa 1780.
Leeds City Art Gallery and Temple Newsam House. See page 15
42B. *Creamware plate, pale cream.*
Mark, 'LEEDS∗POTTERY' *impressed. Diam.* 10 in. *Circa* 1780.
Donald Towner. See pages 22, 87

43A. *Plate, pale cream; portrait of the first Duke of Marlborough,*
after Kneller, enamelled in sepia, other decoration in purple and gold.
Diam. 9¾ in. Leeds. Circa 1775.
Donald Towner. See page 21
43B. *Plate, deep cream, decorated in gold.*
Diam. 9¼ in. Leeds. Circa 1770.
Donald Towner. See page 21

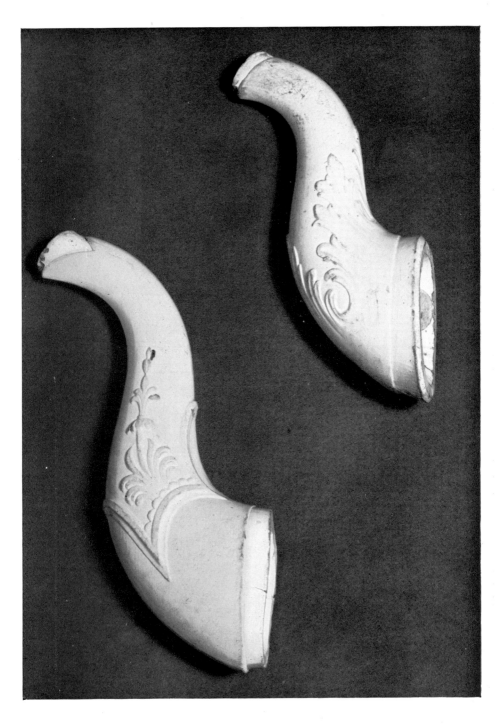

44. *Creamware moulds for spouts from the Leeds Pottery, pale cream.*
Lengths 6 in., 5½ in. Circa 1775.
Leeds City Art Gallery and Temple Newsam House. See page 66

45. *Saltglaze mould for wall vase from the Leeds Pottery.*
Circa 1775. *Cf. Plate* 72. *Height* 12¾ *in.*
Leeds City Art Gallery and Temple Newsam House. See pages 15, 28

46. *Food warmer with candle holder, pale cream, uncoloured.*
Height 11 in. Leeds. Circa 1775.
Cf. W. B. Honey, 'Wedgwood Ware' Plate 21.
Donald Towner

47. *Punch-kettle, and stand for charcoal, pale cream, uncoloured.*
Height of kettle 8¾ in. Height of stand 5⅞ in.
Leeds. Circa 1775.
Leeds City Art Gallery and Temple Newsam House

48. *Centre-piece, pale cream. Height 24 in. Leeds. Circa 1775.*
Donald Towner. See page 21

49. *Centre-piece, pale cream. Height* 25 *in. Leeds. Circa* 1775.
Fitzwilliam Museum, Cambridge. See page 21

50A. *Candlesticks, pale cream:*
(i) *Height* 10¼ *in. Staffordshire. Perhaps Whieldon. Circa 1770.*
See page 8
(ii) *Height* 11¼ *in. Leeds. Circa 1775.*
(iii) *Height* 10¾ *in. Leeds. Circa 1775.*
Donald Towner
50B. *Flask, pale cream, uncoloured. Length* 6¾ *in. Leeds. Circa 1775.*
Donald Towner

51A. *Chestnut-basket and stand, pale cream, uncoloured.*
Height 8⅝ in. Diam. 9⅞ in. Leeds. Circa 1780.
Victoria and Albert Museum. See pages 17, 21
51B. *Tureen, pale cream, painted in underglaze blue.*
Height 9¼ in. Length 14 in. Leeds. Circa 1780.
Donald Towner. See page 19

52A. *Tea-pot, pale cream, decorated with stripes of green under the glaze. Height $4\frac{1}{4}$ in. Leeds. Circa 1775.*
Donald Towner. See page 20

52B. (i) *Pair of egg-cups, pearl ware, decorated with green under the glaze. Height $2\frac{3}{4}$ in. Leeds. Circa 1785.*

(ii) *Cream-jug, pale cream, decorated with stripes of green under the glaze. Height 3 in. Leeds. Circa 1775.*
Donald Towner. See page 20

53A. *Figure of a fox, decorated with touches of green and yellow under the glaze. Height* 3¼ *in. Length* 4½ *in. Leeds. Circa* 1775.
Mrs. Robert Sargeant. See page 22

53B. *Figures of cocks, decorated with touches of green under the glaze, the centre one with grey. Height* 3 *in.* 3½ *in.* 3 *in. Leeds. Circa* 1775.
Mrs. Robert Sargeant. See page 22

54. *Group, decorated with green and brown under the glaze.*
Height 7½ in. Cf. applied flowers with Leeds flower knob.
Appendix I, Plate V, fig. 4C. Leeds. Circa 1775.
Victoria and Albert Museum. See pages 22, 70

55. *Figure, sometimes called 'Prince Rupert' or 'Hamlet' decorated with green and brown under the glaze. Height 12¾ in. (the same floral reliefs occur on other pieces of Leeds pottery). Leeds. Circa 1775 Mr. and Mrs. Victor Gollancz. See page 22*

56. *Figure, from a pair of falconers, pearlware, enamelled in yellow,*
dark red, turquoise, brown, and black.
Height 7¼ in. Mark, 'LEEDS POTTERY.' impressed. Circa 1785.
See Plate 57.
British Museum. See pages 22, 33, 87

57. *Figure, a falconer, pearlware, Height, 7½ in.*
Mark, 'LEEDS POTTERY.' *impressed. Circa 1785.*
Leeds City Art Gallery and Temple Newsam House. See page 23

58. *Figure of Andromache, pearlware, enamelled in yellow, green,
red, pink and blue. Height* 11¾ *in.*
Mark, 'LEEDS POTTERY.' *impressed. Circa* 1790.
Victoria and Albert Museum. See page 23

59. *Figure, emblematic of 'Air', pearlware, enamelled in dark red, purple, grey-brown and flesh-colour.*
Height 6¼ in. Mark, 'LEEDS POTTERY.' *impressed twice.*
Circa 1790.
Donald Towner. See page 23

60. *Masonic jug, transfer printed in black with the arms of the Moderns between two Wardens, the Master seated above, the motto 'Amor honor et justitia' on a scroll. A hunting scene on the reverse, the letters J. B. inscribed in front; enamelled over the transfer in red, yellow, and green. Height 8 in. Mark, 'Leeds Pottery' in the print. Circa 1780. (Probably made for John Barwick, a partner in the Leeds Pottery in 1781.)*

Mr. and Mrs. Victor Gollancz. See pages 21, 89

61. *Coffee-pot, transfer printed in purplish black*
depicting two allegories. Mark, 'Leeds Pottery'
in the print. Height 9 in. Circa 1785.
Victoria and Albert Museum. See pages 20, 21, 89

62A. *Teapot, transfer printed in brick red; a rose on one side, a flute player and two children dancing on the reverse, butterflies on the cover.*
Height 5½ in. Leeds or Swinton. Circa 1780.
Donald Towner. See page 44

62B. *Punch-kettle, transfer printed in black, showing 'May-day' engraved by Robert Hancock and on the reverse 'Harlequin and Columbine', butterflies on the cover.*
Height 8¼ in. Leeds. Circa 1775.
Mr. and Mrs. Victor Gollancz. See page 20

63A. *Teapot, transfer printed in black, enamelled over in iridescent green. Flowers on the reverse, insects on the cover.*
Height 5¼ in. Probably Leeds. Circa 1780.
Mr. and Mrs. Victor Gollancz. See page 71
63B. *Punch-kettle, transfer printed in black, enamelled over in iridescent green, traces of gilding. Flowers on the reverse, butterflies on the cover. Height 9 in. Probably Leeds. Circa 1780.*
Mr. and Mrs. Victor Gollancz

64A. *Teapot, enamelled in red, green, purple, yellow and black, showing 'Aurora'; and on the reverse, the sun rising behind a landscape between two cherubs. Height 5¾ in. Leeds. Circa 1775.*
Donald Towner. See pages 24, 31, 66

64B. *Teapot, enamelled in red, green, blue, black, yellow, pink and turquoise. Height 4¼ in. Leeds. Circa 1775.*
Castle Museum Norwich. See page 24

65A. *Teapot, transfer printed in black from an engraving by William Greatbatch, enamelled over in red, green, purple, yellow and black, showing 'Aurora'; and on the reverse, the world between the sun and moon.*

Height 4¼ in. Probably Leeds. Circa 1780.
Victoria and Albert Museum. See pages 30, 32, 66

65B. *Teapot, transfer printed in black from an engraving by William Greatbatch, enamelled over in red, green, purple and yellow, and inscribed 'The Hon'ble. Aug'tus Keppel'; on the reverse, a man of war in full sail. Height 5¼ in. Probably Leeds. Circa 1780.*
Donald Towner. See pages 30, 32

66A. *Teapot, transfer printed in black from an engraving by William Greatbatch, enamelled over in red, green, yellow and rosy-purple, inscribed 'The Prodigal Son in Excess'; on the reverse 'The Prodigal Son in Misery'. Height* 4¾ *in. Probably Leeds. Circa* 1780.
See pages 24, 30

66B. *Teapot, transfer printed in black from an engraving by William Greatbatch, enamelled over in red, green, yellow and rosy-purple. Inscribed 'The XII Houses of Heaven' and 'Published as the Act directs Jan'y.* 4, 1778 *by W. Greatbatch, Lane Delf, Staffordshire'; on the reverse 'The Fortune Teller'. Height* 5 *in. Probably Leeds. Mr. and Mrs. Victor Gollancz. See pages* 30, 32, 66, 91

67A. *Teapot, transfer printed in black from an engraving by William Greatbatch, enamelled over in red, green, yellow and rosy-purple, 'Captain Cook being directed by Brittania', and inscribed 'WRO No. 129'; on the reverse the world between sun and moon, etc. Height $5\frac{3}{4}$ in. Probably Leeds. Circa 1780. Donald Towner. See pages 30, 32*

67B. *Teapot, transfer printed in black from an engraving by William Greatbatch, enamelled over in green, yellow, rosy-purple and black inscribed 'The Prodigal Son receives his Patrimony'; on the reverse 'The Prodigal Son taking leave'. Height $6\frac{1}{4}$ in. Origin uncertain, perhaps Leeds or Swinton. Circa 1780. Donald Towner.*
See pages 30, 31, 32

68. *Chocolate-jug and stand, pearl ware, enamelled in brown and purple. 'GFK' inscribed in monogram. Mark, 'LEEDS✶POTTERY'. impressed. Height of jug 5 in. Length of stand 6½ in. Circa 1790. Mr. and Mrs. Victor Gollancz. See pages 19, 24*

69. *Vase, uncoloured. Mark,* 'LEEDS . POTTERY' *impressed.*
Height 10¾ *in. Made at Leeds. Circa* 1915.
Fitzwilliam Museum Cambridge. See page 89

70. *Saltglaze mould for teapot or tea-caddy. Height $3\frac{3}{4}$ in. Probably made by William Greatbatch for either Whieldon or Wedgwood. Circa 1760.*
Victoria and Albert Museum. See page 27

71A. *Creamware teapot, enamelled in red, yellow, green and black. Height 5 in. Probably made by William Greatbatch for Wedgwood in 1764. Cf. Plate 70.*
Donald Towner. See pages 26, 29, 35
71B. *Creamware teapot, enamelled in red, yellow, green, rosy-purple and black. Height 5¾ in.*
Probably made by William Greatbatch for Wedgwood in 1764. Cf. Plate 70.
Donald Towner. See pages 26, 29, 35

72. *Saltglaze wall vase 'Flora'. Height* 11½ *in.*
Probably made by William Greatbatch for Whieldon or Wedgwood.
Circa 1760. *Cf. Plate* 45.
Trustees of T. M. Ragg. See page 28

73. *Creamware tea-caddy 'Flora' with silver cover.*
Height 6½ in. Probably William Greatbatch.
Circa 1765. Cf. Plates 45 and 72.
Donald Towner. See page 28

74. *Coffee-pot, deep cream, transfer printed, in red at Liverpool;*
'Tea Party' on reverse.
Height 8¾ in. Wedgwood. Circa 1763.
Donald Towner. See page 41

75A. *Sugar-bowl, deep cream, transfer printed in red.*
Diam. 4¾ in. Wedgwood. Circa 1763.
Teapot, paler cream, transfer printed in black at Liverpool.
Height 5¾ in. Wedgwood. Circa 1765.
Victoria and Albert Museum. See page 65
75B. *Teapot, paler cream, transfer printed in black at Liverpool.*
Height 7 in. Wedgwood. Circa 1764.
British Museum. See page 65

76A. *Teapot, pale cream, enamelled in red, black,*
purple, green and yellow by D. Rhodes.
Height 4¾ in. Wedgwood. Circa 1768.
(The cover is a replacement of Leeds manufacture.)
Victoria and Albert Museum. See page 37
76B. *Teapot, pale cream, enamelled in red, black,*
purple, green and yellow by D. Rhodes.
Height 4½ in. Mark, 'WEDGWOOD' impressed. Circa 1770.
Donald Towner. See pages 37, 68, 94

77A. *Teapot, pale cream, enamelled in red, black,
purple, green and yellow by D. Rhodes.
Height 5½ in. Wedgwood. Circa 1766.
Donald Towner. See pages 28, 66*
77B. *Teapot, pale cream, enamelled in red, black,
purple, green and yellow by D. Rhodes.
Inscribed on the reverse 'Success to Sir Charles Holte Esq'.
Height 5½ in. Wedgwood. 1774.
Norwich Castle Museum. See page 37*

78A. *Teapot, pale cream, enamelled in red, black,*
purple, green and yellow and pink by D. Rhodes.
Height 4¾ in. Wedgwood. Circa 1766.
Trustees of T. M. Ragg
78B. *Teapot, reverse of Plate 76A. See page 37*

79A. *Teapot, deep cream, enamelled in red, black,*
blue, yellow, pink, and green; painted by D. Rhodes.
Height 6 in. Wedgwood. Circa 1764.
Norwich Castle Museum. See page 38
79B. *Teapot, pale cream, enamelled in red, black,*
purple, blue, green and yellow, perhaps painted by J. Bakewell.
Height 4½ in. Mark, 'WEDGWOOD' impressed. Circa 1775.
Donald Towner. See pages 18, 35, 38, 94

80A. *Teapot, pale cream, enamelled in red, black,
purple, green and pink, by D. Rhodes.
Height 5 in. Wedgwood. Circa 1775.
Mr. and Mrs. Victor Gollancz. See page 38*
80B. *Teapot, pale cream, enamelled in red, black,
purple, green and yellow by D. Rhodes.
Height 5½ in. Wedgwood. Circa 1775.
Trustees of T. M. Ragg. See page 38*

81. *Coffee-pot, pale cream, enamelled in red, black,*
purple, green and yellow by D. Rhodes.
Height 10 in. Wedgwood. Circa 1775.
Trustees of T. M. Ragg. See pages 38, 65, 69, 94

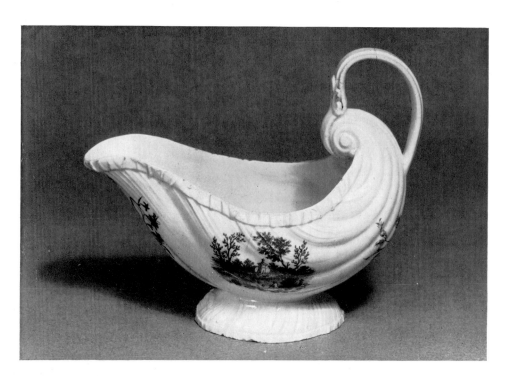

82A. *Sauce-boat, deep cream, transfer printed in purple by Sadler and Green. Length 6½ in. Height 5½ in. Wedgwood. Circa 1764.*
Mrs. R. Sargeant. See page 41

82B. *Teapot, pale cream, transfer printed in black from an engraving by W. Greatbatch, enamelled in red, black, green, rose, and yellow. Height 5 in. Wedgwood. Circa 1775.*
Victoria and Albert Museum. See pages 31, 32

83A. *Bowl, pale cream, transfer printed in black by Sadler and Green.*
Diam. 8 in. Height $5\frac{1}{2}$ in. Mark, 'WEDGWOOD' impressed.
Circa 1770.
Donald Towner. See page 41
83B. *Teapot, pale cream, transfer printed in black.*
Mark, 'Green, Liverpool' in the print, an incised cross underneath.
Height $4\frac{3}{4}$ in. Wedgwood. Circa 1775.
Donald Towner. See pages 21, 98

84. *Covered jug, pale cream, transfer printed in deep red with the 'Tea party' depicting Josiah and Sarah Wedgwood drinking tea, 'The Shepherd', on the reverse.*
Height 5¾ in. Mark, 'WEDGWOOD' impressed. Circa 1775.
Donald Towner. See pages 41, 95

85. *Coffee-pot, pale cream, transfer printed in black,*
enamelled over in two shades of green; traces of gilding.
Decorated by Green, Liverpool. Height $8\frac{1}{2}$ in.
Mark, 'WEDGWOOD' impressed. Circa 1777.
Donald Towner. See pages 28, 39, 65, 94

86A. *Sweetmeat dish, deep cream, enamelled in purple.*
Length 7¾ in. Marks, 'G' in purple and 'WEDGWOOD' impressed.
Circa 1765.
Victoria and Albert Museum. See page 38
86B. *Plate, deep cream, enamelled in black and yellow,*
probably by J. Bakewell. Diam. 8½ in. Wedgwood. Circa 1765.
Donald Towner. See page 38

87A. *Cup and saucer, pale cream, gilded decoration.*
Height of cup 2¼ *in. Diam. of saucer* 4¾ *in.*
Mark, 'WEDGWOOD' impressed. Circa 1768.
Donald Towner. See page 69

87B. *Plate, pale cream, enamelled in red, yellow, green, purple,*
crimson and grey; crimson coloured edging.
Perhaps decorated at Liverpool. Diam. 9 *in. Wedgwood. Circa* 1780.
Donald Towner. See page 39

88A. *Plate, deep cream, transfer printed in dark red*
by Sadler and Green.
Diam. $9\frac{1}{2}$ in. Wedgwood. Circa 1765.
Donald Towner. See page 41
88B. *Teapot, pale cream, transfer printed in black*
by Green, Liverpool. Height $5\frac{1}{2}$ in.
Mark, 'WEDGWOOD'. Circa 1780.
Fitzwilliam Museum, Cambridge. See page 71

89. *Jug, pale cream, transfer printed in black*
by Green, Liverpool. Height 13¼ *in. Wedgwood. Circa 1785.*
Donald Towner. See page 41

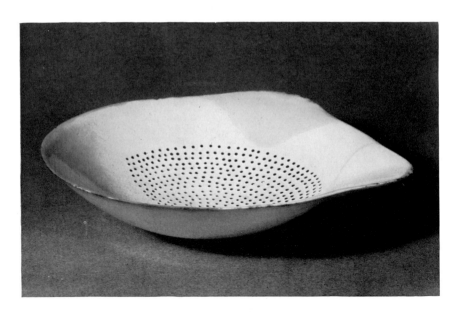

90A. *Skimmer, pale cream, uncoloured, length* 7¾ *in.*
Mark, 'WEDGWOOD' impressed. Circa 1785.
Miss Margaret Thomas. See page 81
90B. *Butter-dish, pale cream, uncoloured.*
Height 3½ *in. Diam.* 5¾ *in. Mark, 'WEDGWOOD' impressed.*
Circa 1785.
Victoria and Albert Museum. See page 71

91A. *Cake-basket, pale cream, enamelled in turquoise and gilded.*
Height 7¾ in. Mark, 'WEDGWOOD' impressed. Circa 1790
Victoria and Albert Museum. See pages 71, 94
91B. *Tureen, pale cream, enamelled in brown, green, and purple;*
enamelled inscription added in Holland.
Diam. 12 in. Mark, 'WEDGWOOD' impressed. Circa 1790.
Victoria and Albert Museum. See pages 40, 42

92A. *Teapot, deep cream, enamelled in black, green and purple.*
Height 3¾ in. Probably Liverpool. Circa 1765.
Donald Towner. See page 54

92B. *Bowl, pale cream, enamelled in apple-green, rosy-purple, blue,*
orange-red, yellow and black.
Diam. 6 in. Liverpool. Circa 1780.
Donald Towner. See page 59

93A. *Plate, pale cream, enamelled by a Dutch painter in red, rosy-purple, green, yellow, brown, blue and black. Diam. 8 in. Liverpool.*
Circa 1785.
Donald Towner

93B. *Teapot, pale cream, transfer printed in reddish brown.*
Engraving by Richard Abbey. Height 6½ in.
Mark, 'Abbey' in the print. Liverpool. Circa 1780.
Fitzwilliam Museum, Cambridge. See page 55

94A. *Figures of Spring and Summer, pale cream,*
enamelled in various colours. Height 5½ in.
Figure of Spring marked, 'Neale & Co.', impressed. Circa 1780.
Fitzwilliam Museum, Cambridge. See page 48
94B. *Figures of Autumn and Winter, pale cream,*
enamelled in various colours. Height 5½ in. Circa 1780.
Fitzwilliam Museum, Cambridge. See page 48

95A. *Plate, pale cream, transfer printed*
and enamelled in red, green, blue and yellow.
Diam. 9½ *in. Mark,* 'NEALE & CO.' *Circa* 1780.
Donald Towner. See page 48
95B. *Cup and saucer, pale cream, enamelled in emerald green.*
Height of cup 2 *in. Diam. of saucer* 4¾ *in. Neale and Co. Circa* 1775.
Donald Towner. See page 48

96A. *Plate, pale cream, enamelled in Holland,*
in red, purple-brown, green and yellow.
Diam. 10 in. Mark, 'TURNER', impressed. Circa 1780.
Donald Towner. See pages 19, 98
96B. *Mugs, pale cream; 1, transfer printed in umber and enamelled*
over in blue, red, yellow, green and brown.
Height 4⅝ in. Mark in the print, 'Bristol Pottery 1802'. See page 57
E. N. Stretton.
2, transfer printed in yellow, green, purple, orange and brown.
Height 5¼ in. Bristol Pottery. Circa 1800. See page 30.
E. N. Stretton